Clever, Kind, Tricky, and Sly

A Bulgarian Folktale Sampler

"Priscilla Howe's delightful book of 43 Bulgarian folktales is more than an anthology. Through Howe's background in languages, libraries—and most important, storytelling—the book unfolds like a performance. She shapes these retellings with her storyteller's power of verbal repetition, reversal, and sound effects. Howe contextualizes and comments on the funny, wry, and whimsical tales in introductions that tell her own stories of visiting and living in Bulgaria. Readers will be captivated by her enchanting tales of playing an American folk tune on harmonica with a Bulgarian street performer, following the strict rules in archives, being caught in a street full of cats, buying seasonal food at markets, and competing in a joke-telling and storytelling competition sponsored by the Bulgarian House of Humor and Satire in Gabrovo. (You'll have to read the book to find out what happens.)

—Lori Brack, author of *Museum Made of Breath*

Clever, Kind, Tricky, and Sly

A Bulgarian Folktale Sampler

Translated and Retold by
International StoryBridge Award Recipient

Priscilla Howe

Parkhurst Brothers Publishers

MARION, MICHIGAN

www.parkhurstbrothers.com

Consumers may order Parkhurst Brothers books from their favorite online or bricks-and-mortar booksellers, expecting prompt delivery. Parkhurst Brothers books are distributed to the trade through the Chicago Distribution Center. Trade and library orders may be placed through Ingram Book Company, Baker & Taylor, Follett Library Resources and other book industry wholesalers. To order from Chicago Distribution Center, phone 1-800-621-2736 or fax to 800-621-8476. Copies of this and other Parkhurst Brothers Publishers titles are available to organizations and corporations for purchase in quantity by contacting Special Sales Department at our home office location, listed on our web site. Manuscript submission guidelines for this publishing company are available at our web site.

Printed in the United States of America

First Edition, September 2021

Printing history: 2021 2022 2023 2024   10 9 8 7 6 5 4 3 2 1

ISBN: Trade Paperback   978162491-155-2
ISBN: e-book   978162491- 156-9

Parkhurst Brothers Publishers believes that the free and open exchange of ideas is essential for the maintenance of our freedoms. We support the First Amendment of the United States Constitution and encourage all citizens to study all sides of public policy questions, making up their own minds.

Page design by   Susan Harring
Cover design by   Linda D. Parkhurst
Proofread by   Bill and Barbara Paddack
Metadata management by   Linda D. Parkhurst
Acquired for Parkhurst Brothers Publishers
And edited by: Ted Parkhurst

092021

Acknowledgements

I am deeply grateful to the staff of the Institute of Ethnology and Folklore Studies with Ethnographic Museum of the Bulgarian Academy of Sciences (especially Konstantin, who retrieved my archive requests and allowed me to work in his office), the House of Humor and Satire, the Bulgarian National Library, and the Fulbright Bulgaria, for making this collection possible. I would especially like to thank Tzveta Misheva-Aleksova and her family, Albena Georgieva-Angelova of IEFSEM, storyteller and artist Hristo Neykov, harmonica-player Roman Rimski, and my own dear family.

Contents

One Woman's Journey into Bulgarian Folktales

I fell in love with Bulgaria in 1982, during a summer seminar in the university town of Veliko Turnovo. I arrived there by luck, by loving languages, and by saying "why not?" when offered chances. I studied French and Russian at the University of Vermont and, when I spent my year abroad in Belgium (so confusing, these B-L-G countries), I took as many Slavic courses as I could. One day my professor offered a class in Bulgarian. Why not? My Bulgarian teacher offered me the chance to go on the summer seminar, three weeks of study, and one week at the Black Sea, for free. Why not? I had a great time, then went home to Vermont to finish my bachelor's degree. I returned to Bulgaria to study the language in 1983-84. I immersed myself in the culture. During the Cold War era, there weren't many Americans in Bulgaria, so I rarely spoke English. That proved to be the best way to learn the language.

I went on to become a Slavic librarian, then a children's librarian, until I finally found my calling as a storyteller. In 1993, I took the leap into storytelling full-time. In my travels telling stories around the US and around the world, I began to tell Bulgarian folktales that I had translated. Doing so kept me dreaming of going back to Bulgaria to look for stories.

In 2015, my chance presented itself: I received a Fulbright Scholarship to research stories at the Institute of Ethnology and Folklore Studies with Ethnographic Museum (IEFSEM) of the Bulgarian Academy of Sciences in Sofia. I spent five months looking for animal tales and trickster stories to translate and tell. The folktales in this collection are from the archives of the IEFSEM, the archives of the House of Humor and Satire in Gabrovo, from various printed and online folktale collections, and from friends and acquaintances. The stories from Kuzman Shapkarev's nineteenth-century collection *Bulgarski prikaski i viarovaniia su pribavlenie na niakolko Makedonovlashki i Albanski* include tales from present-day Northern Macedonia. Still, as he labeled them Bulgarian, I've included them (the political issue of Bulgaria and Northern Macedonia is well beyond the scope of this short introduction).

Disclaimer: This is not an official Fulbright Program publication. The views expressed here are entirely my own and do not represent the views of the Fulbright Program, the U.S. Department of State, or any of its partner organizations.

About Bulgaria

Bulgaria is located in Eastern Europe, bordered by Turkey and the Black Sea to the east, Greece to the south, Northern Macedonia and Serbia to the west, and Romania across the Danube River to the north. Bulgaria is approximately the size of Tennessee. The landscape includes mountain ranges (some rounded like those in the Eastern U.S. and some pointed like the Rockies), plains like Kansas, hot springs, and caves like Arkansas. Ancient Thracians lived in what is now Bulgaria and archaeological digs often turn up Thracian gold. The discovery of archaeological sites delayed subway construction in Sofia. The central metro station has an ongoing exhibit of some of the archaeological finds.

Bulgaria as a state was founded in 681 CE, long before many other European countries. The Ottoman Empire ruled the land for almost five hundred years, leaving a lasting Turkish influence. Bulgarian friends often told me that the country is an intersection of east and west, connecting Asia and Europe, looking in both directions. There have been other influences as well: Bulgaria was under Communist rule from 1946 to 1990, closely allied with the Soviet Union.

Bulgaria's past is primarily agrarian, though the cities have grown enormously since the fall of Communism. In 1984, the population of Sofia was one million. It has doubled since then. There has been severe brain-drain as educated Bulgarians leave the country to make lives elsewhere. Bulgaria's recent admittance to the European Union has made it a more international city. In 2015 I was startled to hear English spoken on the streets daily, unlike when I lived there in the 1980s. Many old customs remain: though the habit is changing with contact with other cultures, many Bulgarians still shake their heads side to side for yes and nod them up and down for no.

Fresh fruits, vegetables, honey, wine, yogurt, and white cheese are Bulgaria's pride. Bulgarian food is similar to Americans' ideas of Greek or Mediterranean cuisine. Bulgarians abroad talk rapturously about "real" tomatoes and peaches, those from home. Many Bulgarian city-dwellers still have family or a house in a village, with a garden plot. Bulgarians are proud of the Valley of the Roses, where Damask rose petals are gathered every spring. The rose oil is exported for French perfumes. Flower sellers present their colorful wares on busy city corners. Even gray urban apartment buildings often feature geraniums on the windowsills and balconies. In 1984 and 2015, I bought much of my food at outdoor markets in the city.

At the same time, Bulgaria is quickly entering the technological age, with an educated populace in the cities. Sofia's city parks, metro stations, and most businesses have free wi-fi access. When I told stories in schools in 2015, the teachers collected the kids' cell phones before class. In terms of business, the Bulgarian tech sector is proliferating.

Bulgarian is a Slavic language, related to Russian, Polish, Croatian, etc. The Cyrillic alphabet is used rather than our Latin alphabet. In fact, this alphabet was developed in the First Bulgarian Empire by missionaries Cyril and Methodius, now saints, in the 9th century. These two saints are honored on May 24, Bulgarian Culture and Literacy Day.

In these stories, I've tried to write the words as an English-speaker would hear them, not using official transliteration except in the bibliography. For example, I've written the word for grandson as "vnook," instead of "vnuk" because the word rhymes with *kook* rather than with *luck*.

About the Stories

The stories in this collection are my own translated versions, assembled from the story bones I found in the archives, in folklore collections, and from friends and acquaintances. They are not direct translations but are retellings. As a touring storyteller, I have performed some of these for many years.

During my Fulbright research, I looked specifically for animal folktales and tales of tricksters, but I came across many other stories I thought worth translating. I focused mostly on "bitovi prikazki," that is, "household tales," concerning everyday aspects of Bulgarian life. As I have dug into the process of selecting stories and finding other sources, I've added a few wonder tales, including the Bulgarian Cinderella, Mara Pepelyashka.

Many of the stories here are about tricksters, those clever and sometimes not-so-clever characters that appear in many cultures. I became interested in tricksters in Bulgaria because, unusually enough, there are two human tricksters: Clever Peter, who is Bulgarian, and Nasruddin Hodja, who is Turkish. There are even stories in which the two meet up. There is at times, though not always, a friendly rivalry between the two. One of the other main tricksters is Kuma Lisa, the sly fox. Taralezh, the hedgehog, otherwise known as Ezhko Bezhko, often appears in Bulgarian folktales as the voice of reason.

For Storytellers
I hope you'll tell these stories, not word-for-word but adding your own flavor to the mix, giving credit to the source cited in the text, to the country of origin, and to this book, citing title, author, and publisher.

The Characters

English Name	Bulgarian Name
Bear	Baba Metsa
Cat	Kotan Bey and Kotka in these stories
Cinderella	Mara Pepelyashka
Clever Peter	Bulgarian trickster
Dog	Koocheh
Fox	Kuma Lisa
Granddaughter	Vnoochka
Grandfather	Dyado
Granddaughter	Vnoochka
Grandmother	Baba
Grandson	Vnook
Hedgehog	Taralezh or Ezhko Bezhko
Mouse	Mishka
Nasruddin Hodja	Turkish trickster
Rabbit	Zahyo Bahyo
Turtle	Zhelka
Wild Pig	Gleegan
Wolf	Kumcho Vulcho

On my first day in the IEFSEM archives, I started going through a small card catalog drawer of animal folktales, requesting folders that contained not only stories but songs, legends, and anecdotes. The first story I found in the archives has become one of my favorites, so it seems appropriate to begin with it. As with many of the stories in this collection, I found versions of it in many other sources. I've put them together into this, my own version.

Kotan Bey

Every day, as an old woman did her chores, she'd catch the cat licking butter off his paws. Finally, Baba took her broom and swept the cat out of the house.

"That's it, Kotan Bey! No more stealing the butter!"

Kotan Bey sauntered down the road until he came to another little house. Oh! The cat twitched his nose. The smell coming from the house was wonderful. The cat jumped on the windowsill, then into the house. On the fire was a pot of meaty stew, a pot of *gyuvech*. The cat ate his fill, then curled up on the chair and began to purr and snore, purr and snore, purr and snore.

This house belonged to the fox, Kuma Lisa. She came home from the market soon after Kotan Bey started to purr. As Kuma Lisa approached her house she heard something strange. Was it, could it be, maybe… bagpipes? She loved bagpipes and began to sing. Ooolaylay, ooolaylay, oolaylay! Kuma Lisa's singing woke the cat, whose bagpipe-y purr stopped. The two sat and ate *gyuvech* together. They talked, they laughed. They ate, and yes, they fell in love. They decided to get married, if you can believe it.

The next day, Kuma Lisa went to tell her friends the news. "Guess what? I'm getting married!"

"Married? Who are you going to marry? What's he like?" All of her friends had questions.

"His name is Kotan Bey, and he's, well, I have to tell you, he's a little dangerous. He has sharp teeth and claws, and I think maybe he carries a sword." She had seen his tail and thought it might be hiding a weapon.

"When will the wedding be? We'll bring the feast."

And they did. The bear, Baba Metsa, brought a big barrel of honey, Kumcho Vulcho, the wolf, brought a roast lamb and Gleegan, the wild pig, brought green corn. Zahyo Bahyo, the rabbit, what did he bring? Carrots, of course.

They called for Kuma Lisa to introduce Kotan Bey.

"I'll bring him out, but you should hide, just in case. As I say, he's a little dangerous."

The wild pig burrowed into the leaves under the oak tree, with one ear sticking out so he could hear. Baba Metsa climbed the tree. Kumcho Vulcho ducked under the bushes. Zahyo Bahyo vanished into the tall grass nearby.

Kotan Bey came to meet his beloved's friends. He didn't see anybody. Then he spotted something in the leaves, something twitching. Was it a mouse? He crept up, flicked his whiskers, twitched his tail, and jumped right on the wild pig's ear.

Oieeeeenk! The pig squealed, and that scared the cat, who jumped into the tree, right on top of Baba Metsa.

"He's coming after me!" the bear roared, and she jumped out of the tree right onto the wolf's back.

Oww! Oww!

At the same time, an acorn fell out of the tree right into Zahyo Bahyo's ear.

All the animals ran off. Kotan Bey rushed back to Kuma Lisa's house, and the others went in the opposite direction. They caught up with each other.

"Whew, that Kotan Bey is dangerous," Gleegan said. "He came after me with his knives."

"He almost caught me in the tree. I had to jump for my life," said Baba Metsa.

"He threw a big rock right on my back," said Kumcho Vulcho.

"I think he tried to shoot me in the ear. It was awful," said Zahyo Bahyo. "Kuma Lisa was right. He's dangerous. Let's not go back there."

All the animals went home. And Kotan Bey? For the next week, he and Kuma Lisa danced and sang and ate all the food the other animals had brought.

And that's the story of Kotan Bey.

Storyteller's Note: There are many Bulgarian stories of Kuma Lisa, the tricky fox, as well as Kumcho Vulcho (the wolf), Zahyo Bahyo (the rabbit), Baba Metsa (the bear), and Ezhko Bezhko (the hedgehog). At a daylong workshop I gave in Sofia, a Ukrainian participant told the version of this story she knew as a child; many Bulgarian folktales are common in other Slavic countries.

Readers might be surprised to hear that bagpipes are played in Bulgaria. They are found in many countries where sheep are tended, not just in Scotland and Ireland.

Kuma Lisa, the sly fox, is out to get whatever she possibly can, by fair means or foul. Like so many tricksters, her conscience does not bother her. Taralezh (the hedgehog), otherwise known as Ezhko Bezhko, is often the voice of reason (the zh is pronounced like the final g in *garage*).

The Hedgehog and the Fox

One day, Kuma Lisa, the fox, went to visit her good friend Ezhko Bezhko, the hedgehog. She said, "Ezhko Bezhko, let's pick the grapes from the farmer's vineyard. They're perfectly ripe today."

"Oh, Kuma Lisa, I don't think that's a good idea. The farmer sets pit traps to catch us."

"Ezhko Bezhko, don't be such a worrywart! I have two hundred and twenty ideas on how to get out of a pit trap. Trust me!"

"Kuma Lisa, I only have three ideas."

"Don't worry! I've got my two hundred and twenty. Let's go!"

The grapes were perfectly ripe, juicy, and delicious. They were picking them, picking them, picking them when Kuma Lisa—BAM!—fell into a pit trap.

"Help! Help! Ezhko Bezhko! Help! Give me one of your ideas!"

"But Kuma Lisa, I thought you had two hundred and twenty ideas."

"I can't think at a time like this! Please, please help!"

"Very well. The farmer will pull you out of the trap. Pretend to be gentle and tame. He'll loosen his grip on you and you can run away."

That is exactly what happened. The farmer pulled Kuma Lisa out of the trap. "My wife will be so happy! She can have a new fox fur wrap."

Kuma Lisa rubbed her face on his arm and looked sweetly into his eyes. He loosened his grip just enough that she could jump away.

The next day, Kuma Lisa went back to visit Ezhko Bezhko.

"Ezhko Bezhko, let's pick more grapes. Remember how delicious they were?"

"Kuma Lisa, don't you remember the pit trap? You got caught yesterday!"

"I know, I know, but I've got two hundred and twenty ideas on how to get out of a trap. Don't be such a worrywart!"

"But Kuma Lisa, I only have two ideas left."

"Not a problem, I have two hundred and twenty. Let's go!"

They went to the farmer's vineyard. The grapes were perfectly ripe, juicy, and delicious. They were picking them, picking them, picking them when Kuma Lisa—BAM!—fell into another pit trap.

"Help! Help! Ezhko Bezhko! Help! Give me one of your ideas!"

"But Kuma Lisa, I thought you had two hundred and twenty ideas."

"I can't think at a time like this! Please, please help!"

"When the farmer comes this time, he'll be angry because you got away from him yesterday. He'll hit you with his stick, most likely. Pretend to be dead. He'll throw you into his wagon. Then you can run away when he sets off for home."

That was exactly what happened. The farmer came along and said, "You! I'm not letting you get away this time!" He cracked the fox over the head with his stick and threw her into the back of the wagon. When he set off for home, Kuma Lisa jumped out and ran away.

The farmer didn't notice that she was gone. When he arrived home, he called out to his wife to throw her old coat on the fire, as he had a fresh fox skin for her. After she did this, the farmer discovered that Kuma Lisa was gone. His wife was furious with him. He swore he would get that fox next time.

The next day, Kuma Lisa went back to visit Ezhko Bezhko.

"Ezhko Bezhko, let's pick more grapes. Remember how delicious they were?"

"Kuma Lisa, don't you remember the pit trap? You got caught yesterday!"

"I know, I know, but I've got two hundred and twenty ideas on how to get out of a trap. Don't be such a worrywart!"

"But Kuma Lisa, I only have one idea left."

"Not a problem, I have two hundred and twenty. Let's go!"

They went to the farmer's vineyard. The grapes were perfectly ripe, juicy, and delicious. They were picking them, picking them, picking them when Ezhko Bezhko—BAM!—fell into another pit trap.

"Help! Help! Kuma Lisa! Help! Please, please, give me one of your ideas!"

"I'm so sorry, Ezhko Bezhko. I can't give you any of my ideas. I might need them for myself."

"Oh. I see how it is. We've been friends for such a long time, won't you at least give me a little kiss before I perish?"

Kuma Lisa bent down and stretched her nose toward the hedgehog in the pit. Ezhko Bezhko jumped up and bit Kuma Lisa's nose.

Ow! Kuma Lisa flung Ezhko Bezhko out of the trap, but she herself fell in.

"Help! Help! Ezhko Bezhko! Help!"

"Oh, I'm so sorry, Kuma Lisa. I just used my last idea. I don't have any left."

Ezhko Bezhko went home. And Kuma Lisa? I think the farmer got her that time. I heard that his wife had a lovely fox fur wrap.

Storyteller's Note: This story is known in many Slavic cultures as *The Fox with a Thousand Ideas*. Versions can be found in Aesop and in the Grimm tales as well. I first found the Bulgarian version in a collection at the University of Kansas, at the beginning of my full-time storytelling career. The story works well for audiences over age eight who are developing a sense of morality. The end is still a bit shocking for them.

Many Bulgarian folktales feature a grandmother (Baba) and sometimes a grandfather (Dyado), as this next story does. My friend Hristo told me this story one rainy day in a café in Sofia, with American pop music and the sound of an espresso machine in the background. Hristo knows stories and he knows grandmothers—for years he has been gathering stories, jokes, and songs from old grannies in a village in the mountains. He's a natural storyteller and is committed to keeping the folk tradition alive.

Baba's Rooster

Baba and Dyado, that is, Granny and Granddaddy, were very poor. There was no work and no money. Worst of all, barely any food remained in the pantry. One day, their rooster strutted up to them and said, "Let me go to earn my living."

"What? How can you earn your living? You're a rooster! Stop talking nonsense. Stay here with us." They tried to convince him to stay, but off the rooster went, stopping only to peck at a bug or a worm. He found his way to the castle, where he hid under the cabbages in the garden and began to crow.

"Cock-a-doodle-king! Cock-a-doodle-king! Send me your eldest daughter!"

He wouldn't stop crowing, so the king sent the eldest daughter out. "Ugh, it's just a rooster," she said and quickly went back inside.

"Cock-a-doodle-king! Cock-a-doodle-king! Send me your middle daughter!"

He wouldn't stop crowing, so the king sent the middle daughter. "What am I supposed to do with this rooster?" she said and quickly went back inside.

"Cock-a-doodle-king! Cock-a-doodle-king! Send me your youngest daughter!"

The youngest daughter went out. "Come here, rooster, you can come inside with us." She gave him corn to eat. He wouldn't eat.

The king said, "If he won't eat, toss him in the dungeon."

It was dark in the dungeon, but the rooster pecked around anyway. His beak hit something hard. Gold! He found himself on a pile of gold. The rooster swallowed the gold and hid more under his feathers. When the guards came to check on him, he lay as if dead. The guards tossed him outside the castle walls.

The Rooster waddled home. He said, "Baba, wrap me up in an apron and hit me with a stick, first on the top, then on the bottom."

"How can I hit you with a stick, dear Rooster? I don't want to hurt you." The rooster began to crow and wouldn't stop. At last, Baba wrapped him up and whacked him with a stick. Out popped the gold.

"We're rich. We're rich! Look at all this gold! Thank you, sweet Rooster!"

Of course, Baba couldn't keep this good news to herself. She told the neighbor.

The neighbor had a cat, so she decided to try her luck with the cat. "Off you go to the palace now. The rooster next door came back with gold. See if you can get even more." The cat said, "Do I have to? I don't feel like it." She sat and licked her paw. The neighbor shooed her out of the house with a broom.

The cat went to the gates of the castle and meowed. The youngest daughter came out and fed her a bowl of milk. The cat went home. Her owner was pleased to see her so quickly. She wrapped the cat up and hit it with the stick. The cat yowled and ran off, leaving no gold behind.

Storyteller's Note: This is a perfect story for talking about animal sounds in other languages. In Bulgarian, roosters generally say "kookoorikoo." Like English, Bulgarian cats say "meow," cows moo and snakes hiss, but dogs say "bowwow" or "jaff jaff," and frogs say "kvak kvak."

The next is an old favorite, a story I've been telling for at least 25 years, also about a grandmother and grandfather, that I found in a collection from the University of Kansas library, not from my Fulbright adventure. Americans are most familiar with versions of this story from Russia.

The Turnip

One day, Dyado, that is, Grandfather, went out to pick turnips. He was picking turnips, picking turnips, picking turnips, when he came to one that was huge. He put his hands around that turnip, and he pulled, and he pulled, and he pulled, but he couldn't pull that turnip out of the ground.

He called Baba, that is, Grandmother. She put her arms around Dyado, Dyado put his hands around the turnip, and he pulled, and he pulled, and he pulled, but they couldn't pull that turnip out of the ground.

Baba called Vnook, that is, the grandson. Vnook put his arms around Baba, Baba put her arms around Dyado, Dyado put his hands around that turnip and he pulled, and he pulled, and he pulled, but they couldn't pull that turnip out of the ground.

Vnook called Vnoochka, that is, the granddaughter. Vnoochka put her arms around Vnook, Vnook put his arms around Baba, Baba put her arms around Dyado, Dyado put his hands around that turnip, and he pulled, and he pulled, and he pulled, but they couldn't pull that turnip out of the ground.

Vnoochka called the dog. Yes, the dog, Koocheh. Koocheh put his teeth, grrr, in the back of Vnoochka's dress, in the waistband, Vnoochka put her arms around Vnook, Vnook put his arms around Baba, Baba put her arms around Dyado, Dyado put his hands around that turnip and he pulled, and he pulled, and he pulled, but they couldn't pull that turnip out of the ground.

The koocheh called the cat. Yes, the cat, Kotka. Kotka put her teeth in koocheh's tail, woof! Koocheh put his teeth, grrr, in Vnoochka's dress, in the waistband, Vnoochka put her arms around Vnook, Vnook put his arms around Baba, Baba put her arms around Dyado, Dyado put his hands around that turnip and he pulled, and he pulled, and he pulled, but they couldn't pull that turnip out of the ground.

Kotka called the mouse. Yes, the mouse, the Mishka. Mishka put her little claws in Kotka's tail, meow! Kotka put her teeth in Koocheh's tail, woof! Koocheh put his teeth, grrr, in Vnoochka's dress, in the waistband, Vnoochka put her arms around Vnook, Vnook put his arms around Baba, Baba put her arms around Dyado, Dyado put his hands around that turnip and he pulled, and he pulled, and he pulled, but they couldn't pull that turnip out of the ground.

They were going to give up. Along came a little beetle, a brumbar. He said, "Can I help you?"

They all looked at him and said, "No, you're too small. You can't possibly help."

"I can try."

The brumbar put its little tiny pincers in Mishka's tail, eee! Mishka put her little claws in kotka's tail, meow! Kotka put her teeth in koocheh's tail, woof! Koocheh put his teeth, grrr, in Vnoochka's dress, in the waistband, Vnoochka put her arms around Vnook, Vnook put his arms around Baba, Baba put her arms around Dyado, Dyado put his hands around that turnip and he pulled, and he pulled, and he pulled and at last, they pulled that turnip out of the ground.

It was so big they couldn't get it in the house. They had to cut it up into pieces. They took the pieces inside and made turnip soup, turnip stew, steamed turnip, fried turnip, baked turnip, and turnip bread. And do you know who ate most of it? Of course, the brumbar.

Storyteller's Note: Most Bulgarians know the rhyming version by the author Ran Bosilek, which ends with the mouse as the last animal helper. I like this one, partly because of the onomatopoetic sound of the word for beetle, "brumbar." When I tell this, children usually join in on the actions of all the characters pulling each other.

Not all Bulgarian animals in stories are tricksters. I found this tale of a helpful animal in a collection in the Bulgarian National Library. Using the National Library was an adventure in itself. I took my passport, my other identification papers, and a small fee to the application desk, where I filled in various forms. Then I was assigned a reading room. Before I could go to that reading room, I was required to leave my coat and knapsack in the coat check. I filled out a form so I could retrieve them later. In the reading room, I filled out a slip requesting the materials I wanted. I was using the same periodical every time, and it conveniently was directly behind the librarian's desk. I would take one volume at a time to my seat. My seat number was recorded on the book request slip. Taking pictures of the materials was forbidden, and photocopying was expensive, so I took handwritten notes on the stories. One day as I sat in the reading room, a sound filtered into my consciousness, something I hadn't heard for years: a typewriter in a nearby room!

Turtle Fetches the Water

All the animals gathered for a party. Everyone was there, except the ants.

They were hurrying to get ready for winter. The other animals sent Zhelka the turtle to get the water. She set off, one slow step at a time. At the well, she filled a big pot. She started back, one slow step at a time.

After an hour or so, she heard voices: "Oh, Zhelka, can we have some? We've been working so hard."

It was the ants.

"Of course, have a sip now." They drank all the water, so Zhelka turned and one slow step at a time went back to fill the pot.

"Haw, haw, please Zhelka, would you share your water? I'm so thirsty, all I want is a mouthful."

The donkey looked so sad, Zhelka didn't hesitate to give him the bucket. He drank it all. Zhelka went back, one slow step at a time, but on her third try at getting the pot all the way to the party, she stumbled—yes, she *stumbled*—and broke the pot on the threshold of the house.

"I'm so sorry. This is what happens when I hurry."

Storyteller's Note: I was charmed by this simple story collected in the early 20th century. It will fit well into a program on character education, highlighting kindness. While telling this, the storyteller will, of course, slow both speech and actions to match Zhelka's style.

Many popular Bulgarian folktales are versions of Aesop's fables, as is the next one. Grandmother Bear, or *Baba Metsa*, is a recurring Bulgarian character in stories.

A Bone in the Throat

Grandmother Bear, Baba Metsa, had a feast all by herself. She ate an entire donkey. All was well, except there was one bone stuck in her throat. She went to Kumcho Vulcho, the wolf, to ask for help getting it out.

"Baba Metsa, you ate the whole donkey all at once?"

"I was hungry!"

"Hmph. You should have begun by gnawing on the legs, then the rump roast, and on up. Go ask Kuma Lisa. That fox is always getting chicken bones caught in her throat."

Kuma Lisa said, "Oh, Baba Metsa, I can't help you. When I get bones caught in my throat, I ask the stork for help."

The bear went to visit the stork, who said, "I can help you, but what will you pay me?"

"I'll tell you as soon as you get this bone out."

The stork put her head right in Baba Metsa's mouth, and with her long beak pulled out the offending bone.

"Now, what will you give me as a tip for getting the bone out?"

"I already gave you the biggest tip of all! I let you live, even though I was tempted to eat you up when you put your head in my mouth."

The stork wasted no time flying away from the jaws of the bear.

Storyteller's Note: In Aesop, this story is about a fox and a crane, rather than a bear and a stork, but it is essentially the same. It's one of many Bulgarian teaching tales, though there is no explicit moral at the end as in collections of Aesop's fables.

The next story is a chain story, almost a circle, the end of which nearly brings the listener back to the beginning. This was the first story I found in which the sun is a real character.

Who Is the Best?

Once a mouse wanted to marry her son off, but she insisted on a daughter-in-law who was of the very best quality. She asked all her friends, "Who is even better than I am?" The other animals conferred, and one spoke up. "The sun is the best of all."

The mouse went to speak with the sun. "Sun, do you know why I've come? I heard that you are the best of all. I'd like your daughter to marry my son."

"I'm sorry to disappoint you. I am not the best of all."

"Who is better, then, dear Sun?"

"The cloud is better than I am. I can do nothing about a cloud, no matter how much I shine. The cloud covers my face. Certainly, the cloud is better than I am."

So the mouse mother went to call on the cloud.

"Cloud, I've heard, especially from the Sun, that you are the best of all. Would you permit your daughter to marry my son? I'd like him to marry the very best quality."

"Oh, but I'm not the best of all. There is one better than I, the wind. I can do nothing against the wind."

The mouse mother went to the wind.

"No, I'm not the best of all. You see, the shape of the valley pushes me. The valley is better than I."

The mouse mother went to the valley.

"I, the best of all? Never! The river cuts right through me."

The mouse mother went to the river.

"I wish I were the best of all, but the river bank holds me in. The riverbank is surely the best."

The mouse mother went to the bank.

"No, if I were the best of all, I wouldn't be eaten away by the mole."

The mouse mother went to the mole.

"Mole, I am searching for a wife for my son, one who is the best of all. I've been to the sun, who sent me to the cloud. The cloud sent me to the wind. The wind sent me to the valley. The valley sent me to the river. The river sent me to the riverbank. The riverbank sent me to you. I believe you are the best of all. Would you allow your daughter to marry my son?"

The mole agreed and so the mouse son and the mole daughter were married. At the wedding, the mouse mother saw how well her son and the mole daughter looked together. "She even has the same sort of coat as we have. Why did I go looking to those others, when it was clear that she, who resembles mice so much, was clearly the best?"

Storyteller's Note: This story is a twist on the familiar tale of the stonecutter, which can be found in Japan, India, France, and other countries. One of my favorite versions of this tale is from Vietnam, in which a cat owner wants to name his cat "Heaven." A wise man tells him that a cloud will cover the face of heaven, so he should name his cat "Cloud," and so on.

While the northeast of Bulgaria is the breadbasket of the country, resembling the rolling wheat fields of Kansas, much of the rest of the country is wooded and mountainous. Mount Vitosha is snuggled up next to Sofia, a short city bus ride away. Many of my Bulgarian friends are mountain climbers, hikers, and skiers. The word "Balkan," used to describe the region, comes from the Turkish word for mountain chain. It's no surprise then that Bulgarian folklore includes many stories of foresters and animals.

The Language of the Animals

"Help me! Help me!" The woodsman was surprised to hear this voice coming from the middle of the fire he'd built to warm his hands. A snake was trapped on a burning log. The woodsman extended a stick to the snake and carried it to safety.

"Thank you, kind sir! I would like to repay you for your good deed. If you will allow me to spit in your mouth, I will grant you the gift of understanding the language of the animals."

Without hesitating, the man bent down, and the snake spat into his mouth.

"This is your secret. If you tell anyone you can understand the animals, you will die." The snake slid away into the leaves.

The woodsman heard the horses chatting to each other, "Did you see that? I thought our master would die when the snake spat in his mouth."

"It's a good thing he didn't. If we were left out here, we might be attacked by the wolves. I'm glad to be going home. I'm getting hungry."

Back at home, he listened to the dog and cat arguing, to the cow mumbling to the sheep, to the chickens arguing over the corn.

The next day, he and his wife were on their way to visit her parents when he heard the horses talking about their heavy loads.

"You have it easy," said the mare carrying the man's wife. "I'm carrying three, while you're carrying only one."

From this, the woodsman understood that both his wife and the mare she was riding were pregnant. He immediately asked his wife to ride his horse, and he rode more slowly to give the mare an easier journey.

"Why did you ask me to switch horses?" his wife asked.

"I'm sorry, I can't tell you."

Over the next week, she asked him many times a day why he had changed horses. Many times a day, he would not answer. Finally, he said, "If I tell you, I will die."

"I don't believe it. Tell me!"

He didn't answer. She badgered him all day. In response, over the next several days, he dug his own grave. Then he built himself a coffin. He put on his best clothes. He knew he would die as soon as he told the secret.

He was lying in the coffin, ready for his funeral, about to tell his wife about the snake. He heard the dog and the rooster talking.

"What a bully his wife is! I wouldn't just give in like that, not if it cost me my life!"

"I know! He really should save his skin."

At that, the man climbed out of the coffin, thanked the animals, and told his wife he was never going to tell her his secret. And he didn't.

Storyteller's Note: In Bulgarian folklore, snakes are reputed to have riches and powers such as in this story. The word for snake, zmiya, has the same root as the word for dragon, zmey, and there is a belief that a serpent becomes a dragon when it is a certain age.

The return of the storks is a sign of spring in Bulgaria. I came across storks in many Bulgarian stories and finally, in 2015, saw real storks in fields and on rooftops.

Wolf and Stork Open a Tavern

Once a wolf and a stork decided to open a tavern together. All the animals ate and drank there. Most asked to run a tab, to pay their bills later. As summer turned to fall, the stork was anxious to fly south. Kumcho Vulcho, the wolf, said, "You take the little cash that we have, and I'll stay behind to collect from our customers."

They wrapped the small amount of money in a kerchief, and the stork flew away. He saw a pond and flew down for a snack. When he opened his mouth to catch a frog, the kerchief dropped into the pond. From that day on, storks have stood in ponds, looking for the money.

Meanwhile, the wolf stayed behind to collect the debts. Not one animal paid him. This is why, to this day, wolves steal from henhouses, collecting the debts owed one egg at a time.

Storyteller's Note: Another harbinger of spring is Baba Marta, or

Grandmother March. She's portrayed as a cranky old woman who is angry at her brothers Big Sechko (January) and Little Sechko (February), who drank up her portion of wine. If there's a late snowstorm, people say that it's just Baba Marta shaking out her feather bed. On the first day of March, Bulgarians give each other red and white tassels, martenitsi, on pins or as bracelets, in honor of Grandmother March. I've seen giant martenitsi as door decorations. The tradition is to wear them until one sees a stork, a swallow, or a flowering tree, at which point you tie them onto a tree.

At the Institute of Ethnology and Folklore Studies, I met Albena Georgieva-Angelova, a noted folklorist and a fine storyteller in her own right. One of her specialties is the folklore of Christianity, and she has written widely on the subject, including a book with the translated title *When the Lord Walked the Earth*. At the day-long workshop I gave in Sofia, she told this story about the stages of life.

The Span of a Human Life

When God created the earth and all the beings upon it, the man came to him and asked, "Thank you for creating me. Tell me, please, how long shall I live, what shall I eat, and what shall I do?"

God said, "You shall live thirty years. You'll eat whatever you like that doesn't make you sick. You'll rule over other creatures on earth."

"Lord, thank you for the life you have given me. I'm grateful. But only thirty years? Couldn't I have a bit more?"

"Go sit down, and I'll see what I can do."

The bull approached God. "Thank you for creating me. Tell me, please, how long shall I live, what shall I eat, and what shall I do?"

God said, "You shall live thirty years, you'll eat grass and hay, and you'll work hard in the fields. You'll pull carts for that man over there."

"Thirty years? That's a lot of time. Couldn't I have less?"

God called the man over. "Would you like twenty of the bull's years?"

"Yes, please."

"Then you shall live to fifty years of age."

The dog approached God. "Thank you for creating me. Tell me, please, how long shall I live, what shall I eat, and what shall I do?"

God said, "You shall live thirty years, you'll eat crusts of bread and chew on bones, and you'll guard the family and house of that man over there."

"Thirty years? That's a lot of time. Couldn't I have less?"

God called the man over. "Would you like twenty of the dog's years?"

"Yes, please."

"Then you shall live to seventy years of age."

The monkey approached God. "Thank you for creating me. Tell me, please, how long shall I live, what shall I eat and what shall I do?"

"God said, "You shall live thirty years, you'll eat soft foods like lentils, and you'll entertain the family of that man over there."

"Thirty years? That's a lot of time. Couldn't I have less?"

God called the man over. "Would you like twenty of the monkey's years?"

"Yes, please."

"Then you shall live to ninety years of age."

So the man lived the first of his thirty years doing as he wished, living his life as a man. When he was thirty, he worked as hard as a bull in the fields for twenty years. At fifty, he began to lose strength and found he had to work like a dog to guard what he had saved in the previous twenty years. At seventy, he was just like a monkey: he ate soft foods and made faces at the children.

Storyteller's Note: Making silly monkey faces is a universal specialty! I found a version of this story in a collection from the 19th century. Margaret Read MacDonald has a Lao version of this in her book *Five Minute Tales*.

Bulgarian grandparents often take care of their grandchildren while the parents are at their jobs. As there isn't much work in small towns and villages, young people move to the cities. Many older people whose pensions are small have been forced to move out of villages to the city to live near their children. In 2015, I often went to free movies in the afternoons, part of a year-long celebration of Bulgarian film. Most of the audience members were pensioners, looking for something to do or somewhere to rest.

Granny's Bowl

An old woman lived with her son and daughter-in-law, but they never bothered to ask her to eat with them. They slopped her food in a rough wooden bowl. She ate by herself in the corner. One day, the young boy in the family sat carving a piece of wood.

"What are you making?" asked his father.

"Just a bowl like the one Granny uses, so when you and mother are old, you can eat in the corner from it."

The mother and father looked at each other in chagrin and shame. They got rid of the rough wooden bowl and invited the grandmother to sit at the table with the rest of the family.

Storyteller's Note: This story about respect for elders is found in many cultures around the world, from Ireland to Nepal. In some versions, the elder is given half a blanket, and the child saves the other half to use when his father is old.

Another story found in many countries is "Nail soup," "Axe soup," or "Stone soup." Most of these focus on the community aspect of the story, where each member brings something to put in the soup. I consider this version a trickster tale, in which the traveler convinces the old woman to provide the ingredients.

Nail Soup

A wanderer found his way to the house of an old woman, whose family was off working in the fields. She was the only one home.

"Granny, do you have anything I could eat? I've been traveling and am hungry."

"I'm so sorry, my son, all I can give you is a little bread and salt."

"Oh, Granny, bread and salt would be fine. Thank you. If I only had a nail and some water, I would cook you a dish so delicious you would nibble your fingers to get every bit of flavor. If you'll find me a nail, wash it well, and put it in your stockpot over a good fire, you'll see what a delicious nail soup I can fix for you."

"Nail Soup? I've never heard of it." Still, if he would show her this recipe, soup made from just a nail, she could feed the whole family with it when they got back from the fields. She did as he asked.

"Granny, do you by any chance have a bone to drop in the nail soup? We don't need the meat, but a bone would make it tasty."

"Well, there was that lamb we had the other day. I think I could find a few bones."

"Granny, any chance you have a little rice? Not much, just a handful or two. Nail soup doesn't need it, but…"

She was so curious about this soup, she didn't hesitate. Back she went to her cupboard. She brought him two handfuls of rice. He dropped them in the pot.

They sat and talked and after a bit, he said, "You know, a little onion and maybe some garlic would be tasty in the nail soup. But if we don't have any, we don't have any."

"I may be able to find a little bit, my son." She bustled off to pull a braid of onions and garlic hanging from the rafters. She also brought a dried hot pepper.

"Would this be tasty in the soup?"

"Oh, Granny, it would be perfect." He tossed it into the pot with the onion and garlic.

"Most excellent. All it needs is some oil or butter, but if we don't have it, we don't have it."

The old woman, so ready to taste this nail soup, brought him a small lump of butter she had on hand to make the morning pastry.

They sat and talked and soon the nail soup was ready. The man took a spoon and fished the nail out. He tossed it to the side and the two sat to enjoy a delicious meal.

Storyteller's Note: When I visited my roommate's grandmother in a village in 1984, I learned that many rural Bulgarians have a summer kitchen outdoors. My friend Tzveta explained that this kept the field workers from tracking mud and dirt into the house and also didn't overheat the house in summer.

To make this a participatory story, the teller may ask the audience to suggest food the old woman might find to put in the soup.

In English, we talk about "crying over spilled milk," from the old story of the milkmaid who has an elaborate daydream that ends in her spilling her pail of milk before the dream can come true. Here is a Bulgarian version of this.

How a Man Won
and Lost Everything in an Hour

Once there was a man carrying three hundred eggs in a basket on a pole, on his way to market.

As he walked, he said to himself, "If I sell these eggs, I'll have enough money to buy a piglet. I'll raise that piglet—a sow—and she'll have twelve of her own piglets. I'll take them to the forest where they'll get fat eating acorns, fat, fat, fat. I'll take them to market to sell them for a lot of money.

With that money, I'll buy a horse, a white one, such a beautiful horse. I'll ride that horse to the king's palace. Oh, everyone will be impressed, including the king's daughter. Of course, we'll get married and have a son. Let's see, we'll name him Bogdancho. Oh, what a boy he'll be, a fine, fine boy!

One day, I'll go to the market and find beautiful apples. I'll buy one for my son and when I meet him on my way back, I'll say 'Come here, my son, come, Bogdancho, Papa brought you an apple!'"

As the man was imagining all this, he spread his arms to welcome his son. The basket of eggs fell off the pole. He stared at the broken eggs.

"Oh! There go all my riches!" He began to gather the few eggs that weren't broken. He realized there was a man walking next to him.

"Have you been there long?"

"Yes, I've been here from when you gained everything to when you lost everything."

Storyteller's Note: There's an Indian version of this story in the *Panchatantra*, another can be found in the *1001 Arabian nights* and there is a version attributed to Aesop as well. Though I haven't included any in this collection, there are many Bulgarian folktales about a poor man marrying a princess, as happens in this daydream.

It's common for Bulgarians to wish each other "May you be alive and well!" on birthdays and name days (the day of the saint one is named after). Also, on birthdays the celebrant offers chocolates or other sweets to friends, rather than expecting gifts. Here's a joke story I came across in a collection from the 1890s, about being alive and well (or not).

Alive and Well?

One man asked another, "How is everything at home?"

"We're alive and well, only the dog is lying sick on the tile floor."

"What's wrong with him?"

"He was eating the little bones from the mousetrap and he got one in his throat."

"You gave him the mousetrap? Why?"

"We had him carry the gravestone for my mother and it fell on him. It only seemed right to give him a treat."

"Wait, your mother is dead?"

"Yes, she died of grief at the death of my father."

"Your father is dead?"

"Yes, he died of grief at the death of my brother."

"Your brother is dead, too?"

"Yes, he died abroad."

So everyone in the house is alive and well, except that no one is left alive.

Storyteller's Note: This story comes under the tale type called "the climax of horrors" (Aarne-Thompson Z46). The version I was most familiar with before finding this Bulgarian version came from Joseph Jacobs' *More English Fairy Tales*.

Some Bulgarian folktales have a strong moral tone to them, designed to teach the listeners how to behave properly. In this, the lessons of doing the right thing, not being selfish and caring for the poor all come through. Or maybe this one is "what goes around, comes around."

Whatever You Do, You Do to Yourself

There was once an old beggar who, as he asked for food, said over and over, "Whatever you do, you do to yourself." A wealthy woman tired of hearing this from him, so one day, she baked bread with poison in it.

"Here you are, still warm from the oven. I baked this especially for you."

The beggar took the loaf gladly, saying, "Whatever you do, you do to yourself."

He left the town and was going through the forest when he met a young man on the path.

"You, beggar! Do you have any food? I'm so hungry. I'm sure you can spare a bit for me."

The beggar reached into his bag and pulled out the loaf. "Here, take half. A kind lady baked it for me and it's still warm."

"Half? You surely can beg for more. I'll take the whole loaf."

The beggar just shrugged and said, "Whatever you do, you do to yourself." He went on his way.

The young man was, in fact, the son of that wealthy woman. He gobbled down the bread and continued on his way home. By the time he reached his house, he was in great pain. His mother heard him moaning.

"What has happened? Why are you in such pain? Was it something you ate?"

"No, I'm sure not. All I've had today was a loaf of warm bread from that beggar. You know, the one who always says, 'whatever you do, you do to yourself.'"

His mother went pale. She herself had poisoned the bread and now her son was suffering. The beggar's words rang true for her.

Storyteller's Note: I recommend this story for grade four and up, with a discussion afterward. With justice tales like this, I ask the audience what they noticed about a story, as well as how it makes them feel.

At a day-long storytelling workshop I gave in Sofia, my friend Tzveta told this tale, which I later found in folklore collections. She and I had a long conversation about what I think of as the only firm rule in storytelling: "Only tell stories you love." She wasn't sure she loved the story, but she felt called to tell it. Maybe the rule needs a modifier: "…or feel compelled to tell."

The Sun's Wedding

The sun decided to get married. He invited all the animals to the celebration and of course, they all were pleased to come. All, that is, except the hedgehog. Hedgehog found a hole in the ground to hide in.

The sun noticed and went to find him. Hedgehog, Ezhko Bezhko, reluctantly went to the wedding. All the other animals were helping themselves to food from an enormous table. They laughed and talked and ate and drank. Only the hedgehog stood away from the table. Finally, the noise was so great that the lion roared to quiet everyone down. They all felt a great heat at the door and in came the sun.

"I'm so glad you're all here! Eat, enjoy yourselves! It's my wedding day!" The sun walked among the guests. He came to Ezhko Bezhko, who was chewing not the delicious food but a rock.

"What is this, Ezhko Bezhko? You don't like the food I served? Can I get you something else? It's my wedding day!"

"I know, I'm terribly sorry. I prefer to chew this rock."

The sun was puzzled. "Why, when there is this delicious feast?"

The hedgehog shrugged. "I know this is your wedding day, and so I know that once you are married, you will start to have children. You are already so hot, and when there are more suns it will be too hot for the crops in the ground. I am just getting myself used to there being nothing but rocks to eat."

The sun nodded, then turned and left the celebration. He did not come back for a long time. When he did, he called all the animals. "I'm sorry, there won't be a wedding today. Hedgehog is right."

The sun never did get married.

The other animals were furious with the hedgehog, but the sun took pity on him and gave him sharp quills for protection. That is why he has them to this day, and that is also why there is only one sun in the sky.

Storyteller's Note: I found a version of this in which the sun asks God if he, the sun, may marry. God asks the Devil, who says, "Why not? You made the world, you can do anything." God leaves the Devil but is uneasy, so sends a bee to eavesdrop on the Devil. The bee hears the Devil tell his donkey to drink a lot of water, as the sun will soon have children and the world will dry up. The bee tells God, who then tells the sun he may not marry.

Near the end of my time in Bulgaria, I was interviewed on video about my project. This video was picked up by a newspaper website. There were many comments on the piece, so I added my own, asking which folktales were favorites. This next story was mentioned many times. I hadn't intended to include wonder tales in this collection, but this one stood out.

The Neverborn Maiden

Once upon a time, there was a prince who knew that the time had come for him to marry. To find the perfect bride, he had a special fountain built, a fountain that flowed with honey and butter. Women of all ages would come to the fountain to fill their buckets, kettles, and bowls.

The first to arrive was an old woman. Her bowl wasn't quite big enough, so she gathered shards of broken crockery and filled those. Then she gathered eggshells and filled those. The prince watched her from the trees and, without any thought, flicked a pebble at the eggshells. They broke.

"You! How dare you! I curse you, here and now. I declare that you will only marry a neverborn maiden." She took her bowl and bits of crockery and stomped off.

"A neverborn maiden? What nonsense!"

Still, when young women came to the well to fill their vessels, he found fault with each one. He became certain the old woman's curse had power over him. The prince sat alone, despondent, wondering what to do.

His mother asked, "Son, why are you so sorrowful? What has happened?"

He explained about the old woman and her curse.

"Who knows where on earth you can find a neverborn maiden? Only the Sun can tell you, for the Sun travels above us all and sees far and wide. Go to the house of the Sun and ask where you can find a neverborn maiden to marry."

The next day the prince set out in search of the house of the Sun. He went through fields and forests, across streams and rivers, over mountains and cliffs. One day he came to an old shepherd resting by his flock. "Good fellow, can you help me to find the house of the Sun? I must ask him where I can find a neverborn maiden."

The old man studied the prince. "You must truly be in need to have traveled here, where so few pass. Ford this river, then cross the moor. Beyond the moor, there is a flat field. In the middle of that field, you will find a garden and in the garden, a house. This is the house of the Sun, where he sleeps at night. Go well, young man. This is no easy quest."

"Bless you and thank you." The prince went on his way. Indeed, he forded the river, crossed the moor and the field, and there he found a garden. In the garden was a grand house. He went through the gates of the garden to the door and knocked three times. A white-haired woman, bent over by age, opened it.

"Yes?"

"Good day to you, mother of the Sun."

"And to you, my child. This is not a place for humans to come, but since you call me 'mother of the Sun,' you may come in and before the Sun arrives, tell me why you are here."

She led the way into the house, which was fire-bright and gold-sparkled.

"You are sunburned and doubtless tired from your long journey. Sit for a moment, but then don't delay in telling me your story, for I have much to do."

The prince told her all that had happened since he had the fountain built.

"Well, well. This is a place where humans don't come, and there's reason enough for this. The Sun will arrive home tired, thirsty, hungry, and angry. He will certainly burn you. To save your life, I will turn you into a needle and stick you on the back of the door. I'll feed him—I've roasted nine cows, baked nine ovensful of bread and prepared nine barrels of wine—and when he's feeling better, I'll turn you back into yourself so you can make your request."

What could the prince do? He agreed. From his place as a needle stuck in the wood of the door, he watched her set the table.

After a short while, the Sun returned home. He was certainly tired, thirsty, hungry, and angry. He came inside, washed his face and hands, and sat at the table.

He sniffed. "What's that stench? It stinks like a human being in here!"

"How could that be, my son? Eat your supper, you'll feel better."

He ate three of the cows and four of the ovensful of bread, all washed down with wine.

"I still smell it. It stinks like a human being in here."

"What are you talking about? Of course, human beings don't travel this far. Eat a little more, you'll feel better."

The Sun ate the other cows, the rest of the bread, and washed it all down with more wine.

"Very nice supper, mother. Now, I still smell human flesh. Tell me who it is."

"I can't lie to you, my son. There is a human being here. I didn't dare tell you before you had supper." She changed the prince back into a man. The prince bowed his head.

The Sun said, "How on earth did you manage to get to my house? And why?"

Again the prince told the story. "Sir, I came to ask for your help. Because you can see wide and far, I know you can you tell me where to find a neverborn maiden." He explained his search, beginning with the curse.

"Go into the garden behind the house. There you will find an apple tree with three golden apples. Pick one. Cut this apple in half and a beautiful young woman will jump out. She'll ask you for salt and bread. If you give it to her, she will be your own true love. She will be your neverborn maiden."

The prince knelt before the Sun, thanked him and his mother, and took his leave.

In the garden, he found the apple tree with three golden apples. He couldn't help himself. He picked all three apples and set out on the journey home.

As he walked, he thought, "I should only have picked one. The Sun told me to pick only one. This could end badly. But what if the neverborn maiden is only in one of the apples? I should open one now."

He took his knife and gently cut one of the apples. Out jumped a beautiful young woman.

"Give me bread and salt!"

"I have none," replied the prince.

She vanished instantly, to his regret. He continued his journey. As he walked, he began to wonder if that was the only neverborn maiden. He was overcome by curiosity. He cut open a second apple. Again, out jumped a beautiful young woman, this one lovelier than the first.

"Give me bread and salt!"

"I have none," replied the prince.

She, too, vanished instantly.

"I will wait to open the third apple until I am home and have bread and salt."

At last, the prince arrived home. He gathered bread and salt, then in the garden opened the last apple. Out jumped a beautiful young woman, this one lovelier than the other two. She was dressed in a golden dress and her entire being shone like the sun.

"Give me bread and salt!"

He did, and took some for himself. They gazed at each other in deep devotion.

"And shall we be married?" he asked. "I will go for drummers and pipers, dancers and singers, for our wedding procession. Stay here in the garden."

"I'm afraid to stay here alone. I know nothing of the world."

"Sit up in the branches of this tree, where you'll be safe." He guided her up into a tree that overhung a well. He caressed her cheek, then took his leave.

After a short while, a ragged woman sneaked into the garden to fill her kettle with water. She looked into the well and saw the reflection of the golden maiden. Without showing what she had seen, she turned her kettle upside down and pretended to try filling it. "Oh! I can't get the water into my kettle!"

The neverborn maiden called out, "Turn it over. It's upside down."

The woman at the well-turned the kettle to one side. "I can't get the water in!" She looked up. "Please, come down and show me."

The neverborn maiden climbed down and showed her how to fill

65

the kettle. The other woman asked how she came to be up in the tree. The neverborn maiden told of jumping out of an apple and of the prince who had gone to prepare a royal procession.

"Oh, you poor thing! He left you here? Come, let me embrace you." The woman reached out and pulled the neverborn maiden close. She put her hands around the maiden's neck and began to squeeze. When the maiden breathed no more, the evil woman put on the golden clothes. She threw her own tatty clothes and the maiden's body into the well.

When the prince returned, he was surprised to find that the neverborn maiden no longer looked as she had. "Oh, you see," she said when asked, "I have never been in the sun or the rain before, so in the time you were gone, my face became weathered."

The prince was troubled by this but considered it possible. "Come, we shall have a grand procession to the wedding!"

The two were married, and it was not long after that they became the king and queen.

One day, the head of the stables came before the new king. "Your Highness, we have a problem. When the horses try to drink from the well, they cannot. A golden fish splashes water at them each time."

"Catch the fish, then, and take it to the kitchens to cook for our supper."

When the fish was served, the queen turned her nose up at it.

"I do not eat fish."

After the king ate, the queen gathered every bit of skin, bone, and leftover morsel from the fish and threw it all into the fire. All, that is, except for one small bone, which the king took as a toothpick. He retired to the bedroom to rest after the meal. There, he cleaned his teeth and threw the bone into the garden.

On the spot where the fishbone fell, a beautiful apple tree grew up in less time than it takes to say the words. At night, a branch reached into the bedroom, over the bed. It caressed the king and whipped the queen. This happened for three nights, until finally the queen ordered that the tree be cut down and all the branches, leaves, trunk, and even all the roots be burned. She herself watched that it was done.

All but one branch was burned. This branch was tossed aside, under a bush.

An old woman and her grandson came to the castle on that day to beg for scraps from the queen. The boy picked up the piece of wood, pretending it was his horse. He rode his stick horse home. When he was finished playing with it, he threw it under his grandmother's bed.

The next day, the old woman and her grandson left the house, as they did every day. When they returned, the house had been cleaned from top to bottom. The next day, it happened again, and all the mending had also been done. The third day, it happened again, and the front door no longer squeaked. The day after, the old woman hid so she could see who was cleaning her house. She crept in and caught a beautiful young woman, yes, the neverborn maiden, by the arm. "Now I see you! Thank you! Stay and be my daughter."

It turned out the nerverborn maiden was gifted at spinning, so the old woman set her by the window to spin. She shone like the sun, so the entire house was lit up.

The king rode by one day and saw this beautiful young woman spinning. He sent word out to the entire kingdom that the palace needed new wall hangings. He called for all the women in the kingdom to come to a spinning and weaving bee at the palace.

All arrived, including the neverborn maiden. She sat quietly to the side. The king and queen presided over the spinning bee. All of the women sang, each in turn, as they worked. Finally, the king asked the golden maiden if she would sing.

"No, I do not sing, but if you bring me two bowls, one full of seed pearls and one empty, I will tell you a story."

The bowls were brought. The young woman began, "Once upon a time, there was a prince who knew that the time had come for him to marry. In order to find the perfect bride, he ordered a special fountain to be built, a fountain that flowed with honey and butter. Of course, women would come to the fountain to fill their buckets, kettles, and bowls."

As she spoke, she moved a seed pearl to the empty bowl.

"The first to arrive after the fountain began to flow was an old woman. Her bucket wasn't quite big enough, so she gathered shards

of broken crockery and filled those. Then she gathered eggshells and filled those."

She moved a seed pearl to the other bowl.

The maiden continued the story. When she told of being drowned in the well, the young king leapt up and embraced her. "You are my own dear neverborn maiden!"

He caught the false queen, who was rushing out the door. She was given rags to wear and was chased out of the kingdom forever.

The king and the neverborn maiden had a grand wedding. For three days, they all ate and drank and celebrated. I know, for I was there. I ate and drank and celebrated, and what I heard then, I tell you now.

Storyteller's Note: One of the distinctive features of the wonder tale is that the characters are simple, portraying basic motifs without much detail: the innocent neverborn maiden, the evil woman who stole her identity, the thoughtless prince-turned-king. There is, though, character development in this story: the neverborn maiden gains the wisdom to catch the evil queen out, the prince regrets his thoughtlessness. The false queen does not improve but does all she can to hold onto her power.

I found another version of this story about a girl who emerged from inside a cucumber, in a folklore collection from 1896. The ending is my translation of a traditional formula, similar to "And they lived happily ever after."

Many Bulgarian folktales of royalty are similar to those from other European countries, in which princes are required to fulfill quests in order to ask for the hand of the princess. I was drawn to the different flavor of this story, in which the prince is required to find real work before he can even discuss wedding plans.

The Basket-Weaver Prince

Long ago, there was a prince who wanted to marry a certain princess. He sent an advisor to ask the young woman's father for her hand.

This king heard the request, but he smiled and shook his head. "No, any prince who wants to ask for my daughter's hand must come in person. He shall not succeed by sending an emissary."

The prince heard this and set out immediately to visit his beloved's father. He bowed deeply to the king.

"I understand that you would like to marry my daughter?" the king asked.

"Yes, Your Highness."

"Do you have any skills, any kind of trade?"

"Yes, I have all the princely skills. It is through being a prince that I put bread on the table. Your daughter will want for nothing."

The king shook his head, saying, "You may well have all the princely skills, just as I have all the kingly skills. Still, I require that any man who marries my daughter know how to do something of use beyond ruling. Go away and learn a real trade. When you have done so, you may come back and ask again for her hand in marriage."

The young man bowed his head and went home. With all his heart, he wanted to marry this princess. He thought day and night, night and day, of which trade he would like to learn. One afternoon when he was out for a walk, full of worry that he might not find a profession, he saw an old man weaving baskets. As he watched, he became entranced. He invited the old man to stay at the castle to teach him the art of basket weaving. The prince learned quickly and in time could weave baskets that were a thousand times more beautiful than those of the old man. He was able to sell his baskets easily and for a good price every time.

He returned to the king, presenting his finest basket as a gift. "This is the skill I have learned."

"You have paid me and my daughter a great honor. The mere fact that you listened and followed my advice shows you to be a serious man. You learned a skill well. I asked you to do this as fortunes may rise and they may fall, but a man with a skill can always make his living and put food on the table. You may now ask for my daughter's hand in marriage."

The prince understood the wisdom of his future father-in-law. He knelt and asked for the daughter's hand in marriage.

Storyteller's Note: There are a couple of comparable Armenian stories about princes learning to weave. In those tales, the princes are captured and send a message home encoded in weavings.

Bulgaria is just north of Greece, so it's no surprise that there are stories common to both cultures, such as the tale of the king, or in this case the tsar, with donkey's ears. You may remember this from the myth of King Midas.

Tsar Troyan has Donkey's Ears

It happened that Tsar Troyan had donkey's ears. Yes, he was flop-eared. This is why he always, always, always wore his crown, except during his weekly haircut. And this is also why he always, always, always had his barber's head cut off after the haircut. He didn't want anyone to know that he had donkey's ears.

Soon there were few barbers left. It came the turn of a young man, who shook as he entered the tsar's chambers. He knew that his predecessors didn't survive, though he didn't know why. He removed the tsar's crown and swallowed his surprise.

As he trimmed the hair, the tsar asked him, "Do you have brothers and sisters?

"No, I am an only child, my mother is a poor widow."

"I will spare your life, then, if you will promise that you will never tell a soul about my ears."

"I promise. If I break my word, you may take my head."

The young man went home. His mother noticed that he was troubled about something, but he would not say why. Days passed, weeks passed, and the secret weighed on the young man. He spoke little. He slept badly, afraid he might tell the secret in his sleep. He stopped visiting with his friends, afraid the secret would slip out. He was so worried he lost his appetite.

His mother asked what was bothering him.

"I'm sorry, I can't tell you. If I do, I'll lose my life."

She thought, then gave him this advice, "Go deep into the hills, far away from any people, and dig a hole. Tell your secret into the hole, then fill in the hole."

He did just this. He traveled half a day to a secluded spot in the hills and dug a hole. He put his entire head into the hole and said, "Tsar Troyan has donkey's ears! Tsar Troyan has donkey's ears! Tsar Troyan has donkey's ears!" He filled the hole in, wiped the dirt from his hands, and went back home, feeling considerably lighter in spirit.

Time passed, as time does, and a little elderberry bush grew up from the hole the barber had dug. A passing shepherd cut some of the branches to make a flute from this bush. When he blew into it, the flute sang out, "Tsar Troyan has donkey's ears!"

The shepherd played this flute all the way from the hills to the city. People who heard his flute whispered to each other about the tsar's ears. This rumor made it all the way to the tsar himself.

He was furious. He called for the barber.

"You promised me you wouldn't tell a soul about my ears! Why did you break your promise?"

The barber protested. "I never told anybody. I must tell you, though, that I was so weighed down by the secret that my mother was afraid for my life. She advised me to go into the hills, far away from other people, and tell my secret into a hole in the ground. I did this. I promise you, I didn't tell your secret to anybody, but the shepherd's flute has been playing it for days. Go into the city tonight disguised and you'll hear him play the secret. If it's not true, cut my head off."

The Tsar disguised himself as a common man that very evening and went out into the city. He heard the flute playing out his secret.

"Ah, well, the secret is out now. No sense trying to keep it." In that moment, he decided to pardon the poor barber.

Storyteller's Note: An elderberry figures prominently in this story. My Bulgarian city friends gathered elderberry blossoms in the countryside to make a soothing tea.

Laura Simms tells a similar story called "The King of Togo Togo Has Two Horns," and there are other versions from Burma and Wales.

The next story is also a wonder tale, full of magical items and helpers. I had trouble with the translation, as the version I found was written in a heavy dialect. I appealed to my Bulgarian friends on Facebook. In the process, I learned that there is a kind of clay that women used on their hair to keep it healthy. I learned a word for a bagel-like roll, kravaicheh, which for simplicity in the story I call bread rolls. I learned the word for curry comb, used to groom horses. And I learned to beware of talking spoons—in this story, one is in league with the villain. Folktales sometimes follow their own logic!

Little Clover and the Wolves

There once was a mother who had given birth to many girls, all of whom had died, and one son, who lived. One day, when she was expecting another child, she was out gathering wood on the mountain. As she returned, her foot slipped and she fell into a bog. However hard she tried, she could not get out.

A wolf was passing by, so the mother called out, "Wolf, wolf, please help me! Pull me out with your tail, I beg of you!"

"What will you give me if I pull you out?"

"I have nothing, really. If I had anything, I would give it to you, but I have nothing at all."

"Oh, but you will have. You will have a child. If it's a girl, you give her to me. If it's a boy, you can keep him. Promise me, and I'll pull you out."

The mother paused to think. There was no other way to get out of the bog. She thought of her young son at home. With deep regret, she said, "Yes. I promise. If my child is a girl, you may have her."

The wolf offered his tail, she took hold of it, and he pulled her out of the bog. She turned to go home.

The wolf called after her, "Remember your promise!"

Not long after this, she gave birth to a baby girl, whom she named Little Clover. Little Clover grew to be a charming girl who loved to wander in the woods. Her mother had long since forgotten the promise to the wolf.

One day, Little Clover was skipping down the path when she met the wolf.

"Tell your mother I want what she promised me," he said to her.

"I will," said Little Clover, but when she got home, she had forgotten completely.

The next day, the wolf found Little Clover. "Did you tell your mother what I said?"

"No, I forgot."

"You tell her today. If you don't, I will find you and I will eat you up!"

Little Clover ran home and told her mother right away.

Her mother went pale. "If he finds you again, tell him you forgot to tell me."

"Mama, I can't. I already forgot to tell you once. He says he'll eat me up!"

"Try one more time. Tell him you forgot."

Once again, the wolf found the little girl.

"Did you tell your mother?"

"I forgot."

"Grrrr! You tell her that, or next time I find you, I will eat you up!"

Little Clover went home and told her mother.

The mother hugged and kissed her little daughter and gave her a beautiful apple. "There's nothing for it. You tell the wolf that he should take what he is owed."

The next time Little Clover saw the wolf in the forest, he asked her what her mother had said. "She said you should take what you are owed."

"In that case, I'm taking you!" He grabbed the little girl and took her up into the mountains, where he put her in the branches of a high poplar tree. All day, the wolf left her there as he roamed the forest. In the evening he returned and called out, "Little Clover, Little Clover, put down your long hair so I can climb up!"

She threw her long braid down and the wolf climbed up.

Back at home, Little Clover had one brother, Kostadin. He said to the mother, "Mama, where is my sister? Why doesn't she come home? Please, please tell me."

His mother began to cry. She did not want to tell her son what had happened to his sister, but he insisted. Finally, she told the story.

"Where does this wolf live? What mountain does he call home? I'll go get my dear sister!"

"No, my son, no. The wolf surely has eaten your sister. I don't want to lose you as well. Stay here, I beg of you."

He asked and asked, and finally she told him where the wolf lived. He left that very day, in search of his sister.

On the way, he came to an old woman. "Baba, do you know where the wolf lives, the one who carried off a young girl? I'll give you a coin if you tell me."

"Oh, my boy, I do know. The wolf took the girl to a tall poplar.

Every evening he calls up to her, 'Little Clover, Little Clover, put down your long hair' and up he goes."

"How can I find this poplar, Baba?

"I will show you myself." She led him to the tree. Once there, she made a fire beneath it and pulled a cooking pot out of her bag. She put it on the fire upside down.

Little Clover called down, "Not like that, Baba!"

"Eh? How should I do it? Come down and show me, child."

"Baba, I can't. If the wolf comes home and finds me on the ground, he'll tear me to pieces."

Kostadin was hiding behind the tree and heard this. The old woman called up, "I know, child, I know. I want to help you. Your brother has come to save you. Come on down."

"Baba, if I come down and the wolf comes, he'll eat me up and my brother as well, and then our mother will be all alone at home. I don't dare! And if I do come down, the wolf's spoons will tell him where I am."

"I'll tell you what to do, child. You make up some bread rolls and feed them to the spoons, to keep them busy."

Little Clover did this. One little spoon was hiding in the roots of the tree, though, and did not eat the rolls. Little Clover climbed down from the tree and set off with her brother and the old woman.

"Listen carefully, children," said the old woman. "Take this chunk of white clay, this curry comb and this bar of soap. If the wolf follows you, throw the clay behind you. It will make a river of mud up to the wolf's knees. If he gets out of that and keeps following you, throw the comb. A wall of thorns and nettles will grow up in front of the wolf. If he gets through, throw the bar of soap. High mountains will rise up to stop the wolf. This is how you will get away from him."

"Hurry, sister, we have to get back home. I left our mother alone." The brother gave the old woman the promised coin. They thanked her, took the clay, the comb, and the soap, and hurried toward home.

On that day, the wolf had invited his friends, other wolves, to join him at home. "My Little Clover will cook for us," he promised. When they arrived at the tree, he called out as he had so many times before, "Little Clover, let down your hair so I can climb up!"

There was no answer. He tried again. "Little Clover, let down your hair so I can climb up!"

Again, no answer. The little spoon who was hiding in the roots of the tree called out, "Little Clover has run away with her brother."

The wolf said, "Friends, let us run after her. We'll eat Little Clover for supper!"

They picked up her scent and ran fast after Little Clover and Kostadin. When they were dangerously close, Little Clover threw the chunk of clay behind her. Immediately, a river of mud flowed in front of the wolves. The wolves ran right into it, up to their knees. Little Clover and her brother ran as fast as they could.

The wolves pulled themselves out of the mud and continued the chase, getting closer and closer. Little Clover threw the curry comb behind her. Immediately, a wall of thorns and nettles grew up in front of the wolves. Little Clover and her brother ran as fast as they could.

The wolves pulled themselves out of the thorns and nettles and continued the chase, again getting closer and closer. Little Clover threw the bar of soap behind her. Immediately, high mountains rose in front of the wolves. The wolves saw this and turned back, exhausted. They began to argue among themselves and turned on the one who had invited them home, tearing him to bits.

The brother and sister made their way home, where their mother sat crying. She was certain her children had been eaten up by the wolf. They knocked on the door.

"Who is it? Who knocks at my door?"

"Mama, open up and let us in!"

She rushed to the door and opened it, and they all celebrated the children's safe return.

Storyteller's Note: That story has elements of several western European stories, such as "Little Red Riding Hood" (beware the wolf), "Rapunzel" (let down your fair hair), and "Molly Whuppie" (magical items thrown to stop the pursuers).

The Bulgarian Cinderella is similar to many other Western European versions, but it shows its agrarian roots. In the past, young women would gather to spin or sew together, much as in America there were sewing or quilting bees. You'll notice that the guests at the wedding dance the horo, a typical Bulgarian line or circle dance with complicated rhythms and fast steps. I have friends who sometimes go out on the weekends to the "horoteka," a kind of horo discotheque.

Mara Pepelyashka

Once there was a couple with one daughter, Mara. She and her mother would sit and spin by the fire. One day, Mara asked if she could go to a spinning bee with the other young women in the village.

"You may," said her mother, "if you take this wool with you to spin. Take care to spin it all, or I shall turn into a cow."

Mara went off to join her friends. She worked hard, spinning the whole day, but at the end, she still had wool left unspun.

Returning home, Mara knocked and knocked, but her mother did not open the door. "Mother, I'm home! Please let me in." The only answer was a long moo. Mara's mother had indeed turned into a cow.

Not long after, Mara's father arrived home from the market. He, too, heard the moo of his wife. He broke the door down.

They kept the cow well, and after some time, Mara's father decided to remarry. His wife said, "Why are we keeping this old cow? We feed her but she'll never have another calf. Why don't we butcher her for the meat?"

Mara's father agreed. They butchered the cow and made stew. Mara ate not one bite of it, knowing it was her mother. She carefully gathered all the bones and hid them in the ashes of the fireplace.

Day after day, Mara sat by the fire, stirring the bones in the cinders, mourning her mother. Her face was smudged with ashes. Her stepmother took to calling her "Mara Pepelyashka," or Ashy Mara.

Her father and stepmother were invited to a wedding. "Do come with us, Mara," her father asked.

"What would I do at a wedding, Father? I don't even have anything to wear. No. You go on and I will stay here by the fire."

After they left, Mara stirred the bones in the cinders. Suddenly, they transformed into a golden gown and golden slippers. Mara put them on. They fit perfectly. She washed her face and hands and ran to the wedding.

All the guests were dancing the horo. Mara jumped into the line and danced as well and as happily as the most glad-hearted of the guests. Her dress and slippers shone so brightly that no one recognized Ashy Mara. At the end of the evening, she skipped out as lightly as she had skipped in. She ran home, changed back to her old clothes, tossed the golden gown and slippers into the fire and was sitting by the hearth when her father and stepmother arrived.

"Mara, Mara, you should have been there! A beautiful young woman all dressed in gold danced and danced. Nobody knows who she was. What a sight!"

The wedding went on for two more days and nights, and Mara again stirred up the bones once she was alone. Again she stirred the ashes, again they transformed into a golden gown and slippers, and again she went to dance. On the third night, as she was running home across the bridge, one golden slipper fell into the water. She did not stop to pick it up, afraid she wouldn't make it to the house before her father and stepmother.

The next day, a great golden light shone out of the river. The king's horses wouldn't drink there out of fear. The king asked his stablemen if the horses had been watered.

"We tried, your highness, but they were spooked by a strange light coming from the depths."

The king himself went to the river and called for a servant to pull the golden slipper from the water.

"This must belong to the beautiful woman in the golden gown at the wedding. Not even I have such golden slippers!"

He asked all the women in the kingdom to try on the slipper. It didn't fit any of them. "Did every woman try it?" he asked.

His servant replied, "Yes, all but that strange Mara Pepelyashka. It couldn't be her. She doesn't go out. She sits by the fire, playing with the ashes, mourning her mother."

"Try anyway."

The slipper fit Mara perfectly, of course. She stirred the ashes, pulled the other slipper and the gown out, and put them on to become the radiant young woman all remembered from the wedding.

The king asked her to marry him. And that is how Ashy Mara, Mara Pepelyashka, became the queen.

Storyteller's Note: There are versions of Cinderella in many cultures, including the Scottish story of Rushen Coatie, which also features a cow and the ashes. In this Bulgarian story, there are no evil stepsisters, and though the stepmother insisted on eating the cow, she does not seem particularly evil.

I mentioned in the introduction the two human tricksters, Clever Peter and Nasruddin Hodja. Some Bulgarian friends objected to my translation of the name Clever Peter—they thought he should be called Sly Peter or Artful Peter. By any name, he is a resourceful peasant who outwits the authorities and occasionally is outwitted. The Hodja is the Turkish trickster, found in stories in many countries (the word hodja is a title for a teacher), especially areas within the reach of the Ottoman Empire. I'm quite taken with the tales in which the two meet up. Here is one of the first stories I ever told about the two together.

Five Donkeys

Nasruddin Hodja was taking his five donkeys to market. He walked behind them, swatting them gently with his stick. After a while, he grew tired of walking. He climbed up on one of his donkeys and continued toward the market.

"Wait," he thought. "I'd better count my donkeys to make sure they're all here." He began, "One, two, three, four…" He didn't count the one he was riding. "Oh, no, I've lost one!" He got down off the donkey he was riding and looked on the road, in the bushes, in the ditch. He looked back at the donkeys and counted again, "One, two, three, four, five. What a relief! They're all here."

He walked behind the donkeys for a while, swatting them gently with his stick. Again, he got tired, and again, he climbed up on one of them. After a while, he decided to count them. "One, two, three, four." Again, he didn't count the one he was riding. "Oh, no! Not again!" He climbed down from the donkey he was riding and looked everywhere, with no luck. He looked back and counted again, "One, two, three, four, five. Whew."

He climbed up on one of them and rode for a while. On the road, he met his friend Clever Peter.

"Clever Peter, could you help me out? I keep losing one of my donkeys. When I'm on the ground, I count all five of them. When I'm riding, one always disappears. Please, count the donkeys for me."

"I'd be happy to. Let's see, one, two, three, four, five, six. I count six donkeys, but one of them has only two legs!"

Storyteller's Note: This is not the only story in which Clever Peter outwits the Hodja. In one, they agree to a contest to see which of the two is the best liar. Clever Peter tells the Hodja he has to go home first to get his sack of lies. He leaves and doesn't come back, outwitting the Hodja once again.

One of the films I watched during the *100 Years of Bulgarian Cinema* festival in 2015 was a 1960 movie about Clever Peter. It strung together many of the best-loved folktales of the trickster. Here is one of my favorite tales of Clever Peter I was pleased to see in that film.

Hungry Clever Peter

Clever Peter was at the outdoor market on a day when he had no money at all. All he had in his bag was a crust of bread. He walked past the food stalls and stopped in front of one where delicious stews were cooking over open fires. His mouth watered and he longed to order a big bowl of stew. Instead, he pulled the crust out of his bag and held it over the steam from the stew, to soften it and give it flavor.

The merchant at the stall called out, "You, there! Aren't you going to pay for what you've taken?"

Clever Peter answered, "But I've only taken a little steam from your stew. I didn't eat any of your food."

"You admit it! You took the steam! You need to pay me for it."

"So sorry. I don't have any money."

"No money! Tell it to the judge, thief!" A crowd had gathered. The judge came to hear the case. He listened carefully to both sides.

"Yes, I see. Clever Peter, I'm afraid I'm going to have to punish you. Please come over here to this spot." He pointed to a sunny place in the market square.

"Now, I need a stout stick to administer the punishment."

The merchant rushed forward with a thick staff. He stood back with a satisfied smile.

Clever Peter stood still as the judge lifted the stick. He brought it down hard, on Clever Peter's shadow.

"There. Clever Peter has stolen the steam, and his shadow has been punished for it. That's the end of the issue."

The merchant, knowing he was bested, returned to his stall and the crowd went off in all directions laughing.

Storyteller's Note: This story is known as "The theft of a smell" and is found in cultures as disparate as Japan, Peru, Congo, and Italy. Often the judge rules that the smell be paid for with the sound of coins clinking.

In Bulgarian culture, it's polite to arrive with a gift when visiting friends, such as flowers (an odd number for happy occasions, an even number for funerals), cookies, or a box of chocolates. I don't think I ever had a Bulgarian guest who didn't bring at least a small gift. Once a friend came for dinner with her cousin, who had arrived unexpectedly in town. They brought a fully roasted chicken, still warm and delicious. In this story, it's an old chicken.

The Soup of the Soup of the Chicken

A man who had heard of Clever Peter went to visit him, just to see what kind of a man he was. He didn't show up empty-handed but brought an old chicken to Clever Peter, who invited the man in for lunch. Clever Peter cooked up the chicken. The two ate and drank and the stranger went away happy. After a few days, another stranger knocked on Clever Peter's door.

"Who are you?" Clever Peter asked.

"I'm the neighbor of the man who brought you the chicken the other day."

"Well, come in and have a bowl of the soup I made with the leftovers."

A few days later, another man came to visit.

"And who are you?" Clever Peter asked.

"I'm the neighbor of the neighbor of the man who brought you the chicken."

Clever Peter invited him in for lunch. Then Clever Peter brought over a large bowl of hot water.

"I'm sorry if this soup seems a little thin. It's the soup of the soup of the chicken that man brought."

Storyteller's Note: Like many of the Clever Peter stories, this is also found as a tale about Nasruddin Hodja, sometimes told about a hare rather than a chicken.

I love going to the open-air markets in Bulgaria. In the 1980s, I went to the largest market, the Women's Bazaar, from time to time. In the winter, when there were few fresh vegetables, I bought roasted pumpkin or sauerkraut. Spring brought early lettuce and green onions for salad, a delight for those of us tired of winter food. There were long lines for sought-after foods—sometimes I'd get in line before I even knew what was being sold. Back in those days, bananas were rarely found in the markets. They were only sold on International Students' Day, New Year's Day, and International Women's Day. They were expensive. In 1984, International Women's Day was the same day as Shrove Tuesday, before Lent, which in my family meant we ate pancakes for supper. I made banana pancakes that night. My Bulgarian roommate was appalled that I would waste precious bananas. She conceded that they were tasty, though. When I left Bulgaria by train that summer, my first stop was in Austria. Before I bought anything else, I went to a market and bought a big bunch of bananas and orange juice, which was also not available in Bulgaria. Now bananas and orange juice are regularly available. The outdoor markets still sell mostly local goods, though.

Clever Peter at Court

Clever Peter was taking wood poles to market to sell. He carried them across his shoulders and as he walked, he called, "Make way! Make way!" in order not to hit anybody.

There was a man who didn't want to move out of Clever Peter's path. His shirt snagged on a piece of wood.

"You tore my shirt! I'm going to take you before the judge!"

They went to the court and the man explained that Clever Peter's wood had torn his shirt.

"I demand justice!"

The judge asked Clever Peter what happened. Clever Peter said nothing. The judge asked again. Clever Peter said nothing. The judge asked a third time. Clever Peter said nothing.

The judge turned to the other man. "I can't judge the case until I hear from this man. He seems not to be able to speak."

"He certainly can speak! This morning he was calling out 'Make way! Make way!' as he brought his poles to market."

"And you clearly didn't make way? Shame on you for wasting my time!"

Storyteller's Note: One kind of humor is the overturning of expectations. The listener is expecting one verdict and the judge cleverly delivers a different one, for an unexpected reason. We see this clearly in the many stories of a judge rules in favor of Clever Peter or Nasruddin Hodja.

One day in 2015, I visited an American friend in the city of Veliko Turnovo. She mentioned that she had been feeding one of the stray cats in the neighborhood. On a walk in the old part of town, I noticed a couple of cats coming down the cobblestone street. Then there were a couple more. Then more. Soon, there were fifteen or twenty cats running down the hill toward us. Maybe they heard the rustle of a bag of cat food being opened to feed "just one of the strays." I now think of those cats when I tell this story—maybe Clever Peter went to Veliko Turnovo to gather the cats to chase the mice!

The Village of No Cats

Long ago there was a village that was overrun by mice. There were mice in the barns, mice in the houses, mice that dipped their tails in people's coffee, and mice that tickled people's toes and noses at night. There were mice everywhere. One day, Clever Peter stopped in this town. He couldn't believe all the mice he saw.

"Don't you have any cats?"

The people said, "Cats? What are cats?"

"You don't know about cats? They're ferocious hunters. I'll bring you some and they will take care of your problem with mice."

He went to a nearby village and gathered up all the stray cats in a big sack. He brought them back to the village of no cats. In the square in the center of this village, he called all the villagers to come see the cats.

"Before I open this sack, I need to be paid for my trouble." The villagers, though they didn't have much, paid him in all the coins they could. He opened the sack and out jumped yellow cats, black cats, tiger-striped cats, calico cats. They immediately set to work, hunting the mice.

That night, only a few mice tickled the toes and the noses of the villagers. In the morning, only a few dipped their tails in coffee cups. The cats were doing their job and doing it well.

"What a wonder! Cats! Who knew there were such creatures?!"

Clever Peter had a thought. "What if the villagers learn that I've tricked them—they could easily have gathered these stray cats for no money at all. I'd better leave the village before they figure it out."

He set out on the road out of the village, walking quickly. The men sitting in the square saw him leave. "Strange. Why is he rushing away? He looks afraid. Maybe he knows something about these cats that he's not telling us."

A few men started to follow Clever Peter. He walked even faster. They tried to catch up. He started to run. One man called out, "Clever Peter, wait! Tell us, what do cats eat when they finish the mice?"

Clever Peter yelled back, "Meat!"

The men looked at each other. "Me? He said, 'me'! These cats are dangerous! They're man-eaters! They'll eat us up! We'd better get rid of them."

They got their brooms and chased the cats out of town. It wasn't long before the mice came back. There were mice in the barns, mice in the houses, mice that dipped their tails in people's coffee, and mice that tickled people's toes and noses at night. There were mice everywhere. Still, it was better than having those dangerous man-eating cats around.

Storyteller's Note: The repetition of where there are mice is satisfying for young audiences—and for the teller.

Because he's the trickster and well known for his quickness, Clever Peter's friends are always trying to get the better of him. They try and try, to no avail. He always has the last word!

Clever Peter and the Bones

Clever Peter went to a wedding. At the feast, he sat with his friends, talking, joking, eating lamb, and drinking wine.

The other men decided to play a trick on Clever Peter. They piled all their bones in front of Clever Peter when he wasn't looking. Then one said, "Look at all those bones! Clever Peter, what a glutton you are!"

Clever Peter looked at them calmly and said, "I may be a glutton, but not as much as you are—like dogs, you've eaten every scrap of bone and gristle in front of you."

Storyteller's Note: More a joke than a fully developed story, this one shows Clever Peter's cool-headed response, which I'm guessing would be even more galling to his friends.

When acquaintances in Bulgaria heard that I was looking for stories about tricksters, they often started in with jokes and stories about Clever Peter. My friend Roman told this to me one afternoon on the street in Sofia.

Feeding the Clothes

Clever Peter was invited to a wedding. On his way, a horse and cart went by and splashed him with mud, head to foot. He didn't want to be late, so he didn't go home to change his dirty clothes. When he arrived at the wedding feast, he was seated in the corner, away from the other guests. No one offered him food or drink. He sat for a while, watching. Then he left. When he came back, he was wearing clean clothes. The host sat him in a place of honor. Clever Peter raised his glass in a toast, then poured his drink on his sleeve. He picked up a piece of banitsa, a tasty pastry, and smeared it down his front. He rubbed lamb on the shoulder of his jacket.

"Clever Peter! What on earth are you doing?!"

"Feeding my clothes. Clearly, you invited them, rather than me."

Storyteller's note: I love how Clever Peter and Nasruddin Hodja stories straddle the line between story and joke. This one can be found in collections of Jewish, Icelandic, and Indian stories. It is also a Nasruddin Hodja tale.

There are many stories about Clever Peter taking on different professions, like this one about the trickster as a dentist. Bulgarian friends told me about going to the dentist in the old days, when anesthesia was optional. On the night before I flew home from Sofia in 2015, I broke a tooth and had to go to a 24-hour dentist. I was relieved not only that she could fix my tooth, and not pull it as in this story, but that she numbed my mouth beforehand.

Clever Peter, Dentist

"Clever Peter, I've got a terrible toothache. Can you help me? I think this tooth has to come out."

Clever Peter looked in his friend's mouth and agreed to help. "Sit right here and I'll take care of it."

He took a long thread and tied one end to the tooth. He pulled the thread down under the chair and tied it to the rung in back. This chair had a crack in the seat. Clever Peter knelt behind the chair and with a long needle, stuck his friend right in the bottom.

The friend leapt up, the tooth popped out and flew across the room, still attached to the thread.

"Thank you, Clever Peter! I'm amazed you could get the tooth out. It had such a long root I could feel it all the way down to my behind!"

Storyteller's Note: Clever Peter turns up as a poor man, a woodcutter, a dentist, a barber. It seems there's not much he doesn't turn his hand to!

It's a short hop from stories about Clever Peter to stories about Nasruddin Hodja, best known as the Turkish trickster. This is a common one, which includes a feature of many trickster tales: they underline a negative feature, such as stinginess, and balance it with a positive feature, such as cleverness.

Who Do You Believe?

One of Nasruddin Hodja's neighbors stopped by to ask if he could borrow the Hodja's donkey. The Hodja didn't want to lend the donkey.

"Sorry, my donkey isn't here. I lent it out to another friend."

Just then, the donkey brayed in the stable behind the Hodja.

The neighbor said, "I thought you said you lent the donkey out? I just heard it bray!"

"I tell you, he's not here. Who do you believe, me or the donkey?"

Storyteller's Note: There is a similar Iranian story of the time the Hodja invited guests home, but wouldn't let them in after his wife told him there wasn't enough food for everyone. His wife came to the door and said he wasn't home. "We saw him go in!" they argued. He popped his head out the window and said, "Maybe I left out the back door!"

I found the next story in the IEFSEM archives and in some story collections. Again, there's a negative feature, bragging, balanced by a sense of justice.

Nasruddin Hodja is Warmed by Moonbeams

One day in the village square, Nasruddin Hodja was bragging about how easily he could stand the cold. "I'm so tough, I could sleep in that tree tonight with no blanket, no fire, nothing to warm me but the clothes I'm wearing now."

The villagers laughed. "We bet you can't, Hodja, you're just talking."

"A bet? You're on. Tonight, I'll sleep in the tree."

He climbed the tree that evening and slept all night on a wide branch. In the morning, the villagers were surprised.

"How did you manage?"

"Easy, I just watched the full moon."

"Ha! You lose the bet! You had the warmth of moonbeams!"

The next week, the Hodja invited all of those who had bet against him to dinner at his house. This was a rare occasion, as the Hodja was usually reluctant to feed so many friends. Everyone came, crowding into the Hodja's house. They waited and waited for the meal to be served, but they couldn't even smell food cooking.

After an hour, one spoke up, "Hodja, did you invite us for a meal? Will there be food?"

"Oh, yes, I'm cooking the rice now. Let us check on it." They went to the kitchen, where there was an enormous iron pot of water, with maybe twenty rice grains in the bottom, hung over a small candle.

"Hodja! That candle will never heat the water!"

"Right. And moonbeams never warmed a man in a tree on a cold winter's night."

Storyteller's Note: I know this story best as a tale from Ethiopia called *Fire on the Mountain*, in which a poor man watches a fire on a distant mountain to keep himself warm all night.

One of the high points of my experience in 2015 was visiting the House of Humor and Satire, a museum of humor, in Gabrovo. This central Bulgarian city claims to be the humor capital of the country. Every two years, the museum holds the Blagolazh, a joke-telling and storytelling competition. I applied to compete. I sent written copies of two stories I planned to tell, in Bulgarian. I was pleased to be accepted. The Blagolazh began at the museum at 9 a.m. It was unlike any storytelling event I'd ever experienced. First, the children from a local preschool danced and sang for us, in traditional dress (this happens at many public events). Then the children told stories. The kids were seated behind tables with microphones, like a press conference. One by one, they told short stories. The very youngest had help from grownups. The preschoolers danced again while three judges deliberated. After the awarding of prizes, we adults took our seats behind the microphones. I was nervous to perform in Bulgarian, but took a deep breath and launched in when it was my turn. Here's the first story I told:

Nasruddin Hodja at the Bath House

The Hodja decided the time had come to get cleaned up. He arrived at the bathhouse looking scruffy. The attendant gave him a thin sliver of soap, a threadbare towel, and a mismatched pair of bath sandals. He didn't offer to scrub the Hodja's back. After the bath, the Hodja pressed a generous tip into the attendant's hand.

"Thank you, sir, very kind of you, sir."

The next week, the Hodja went again to the bathhouse. The attendant met him at the door with a new bar of soap, a fluffy robe and towel, and the best bath sandals. He scrubbed the Hodja's back. When he was ready to leave, the Hodja gave the attendant a small tip.

"Sir? Uh, sir, was there a problem?" the attendant asked.

"A problem? No, this was an excellent bath."

"Uh, sir, I just wondered...that is...last time you gave me a generous tip and this time, well..."

"Ah! Yes. The tip I gave you last time was for the service today. The tip I gave you today was for the service last time."

Storyteller's Note: In the center of Sofia there is a beautiful old bathhouse. In the 1980s it was still in use, but it has now become a museum. The word for a tip in Bulgarian is baksheesh, a Turkish word which in English has a connotation of bribery rather than gratuity.

The Blagolazh judges asked all the participants to tell a second story, a short one, before they went to deliberate. My second prepared story was long, so it wouldn't do. I remembered a story my friend Roman had told me. I met Roman a month earlier when he was playing harmonica on the street near my apartment. He was playing "Oh, Susannah." I pulled out my harmonica and joined him, to his surprise. We became friends. Every now and then, when I needed a break from work, I'd walk down the street to play harmonica with Roman and listen to his stories. On the Friday before this competition, I told him what I planned to tell, and in return, he told me this tiny one.

Clever Peter's Cart and Horse

Clever Peter was urging his horse to pull a heavy load up a hill.

The horse said, "Hmph. I do not feel like pulling this cart. It's too much."

The cart said, "My, oh, my! I've never heard a horse talk before!"

Storyteller's Note: When school children want to hear a story and we don't have much time, I tell them this, as an example of the shortest story I know. It works best for grades four and up.

There's a much more involved story of talking animals and items called *Talk* from Ghana.

The Blagolazh judges left the hall to decide who won this round. I felt relieved. I was most likely done and could now relax. No. I made it to the next level. I took another deep breath and told the longer story I had prepared.

Nasruddin Hodja Saws the Branch on Which He Sits

Nasruddin Hodja went to cut wood in the forest one day. He was sitting on the branch that he was sawing when Clever Peter walked by.

"Hodja! You're going to fall!"

"I am not. Mind your own business."

"No, really, I mean it, you're going to fall!"

"I said, mind your own business!"

Clever Peter shrugged and continued on his way.

The Hodja continued to saw until, crash! He fell.

He stood and dusted himself off. Then he ran after Clever Peter. "You told my future! I never knew you could tell the future. Tell me, when am I going to die?"

"Hodja, I have no idea."

"You must! You told me that I would fall, and I did. You predicted the future. Tell me, when am I going to die?"

"Really, Hodja, I don't know."

"Please, please tell me!"

Clever Peter sighed. "Fine. Hodja, you are going to die when your donkey has farted seven times."

"Oh, my. Thank you, Clever Peter, thank you."

He went back to his woodcutting, now on the ground. He loaded his donkey up with the wood he had cut and set off for home. Going up a particularly steep hill, the donkey strained, and then, BRAPP!

"Oh, no, that's the first fart. Donkey, slow down. No need to rush."

The donkey made it to the top of the hill, and then, BRAP!

"That's two. Oh, dear." He continued on his way and heard, "Ffffft."

"Three. I'd better make my final plans."

He began to dig his own grave, right in the middle of the road. As he dug, he heard the donkey fart again, BBRRRAAPP. And again, BRRRP. And again, FFFFTTTT.

"Only one more. I'd better get in this grave." He lay down in the grave and crossed his arms over his chest in a posture of repose. He heard the last fart and closed his eyes. After all, he knew he was dead. At that point, a camel driver was taking his wares to market. Camels always wore bells, which clanked and jangled. The Hodja sat up to see what the noise was. That startled the camels. The camel driver came to see what the problem was. When he saw the Hodja in the grave, he began to hit him with his stick.

The Hodja ran all the way home. When he arrived, he said to his wife, "Guess what? I died today. And I have to tell you, the camel drivers in heaven are just as cruel as they are here on earth!"

Storyteller's Note: I've been telling this story for years in a program called "School Inappropriate Stories" (not a problem in this competition, where some of the material was decidedly earthy). The sound effects make this a perfect story for fourth-grade boys.

Imagine my anxiety when the judges asked for another story after that round! I told a non-Bulgarian joke. "One more!" the judges called. I didn't have anymore. Fortunately, they changed their minds after one contestant's story, deciding that there wasn't enough time for more. They conferred, then announced the winners. I won the "Vivid Presentation by a Foreigner" prize. I was the only foreigner.

Later I found this story, which would have gone over well in the Blagolazh.

Clever Peter, Barber

Once, Clever Peter found himself in a village where nobody knew him but everybody had heard of him. He sat in the coffee house at an inn listening to a conversation about himself.

One man said of Clever Peter, "Oh, I bet he's not so clever. Those are just stories. Why, if he were here, we'd show him a thing or two about being clever."

Finally, one of them said, "I'm sick of all this chat about Clever Peter. I'm sure we could all trick him much faster and better than he could ever trick us. Anyway, tomorrow's Sunday and we've got better things to do than sit around here jawing. We've got to get ourselves to the barber for a shave and a trim."

Clever Peter spoke up. "Fellows, I'm a barber. I'd be happy to give you all a shave and a trim."

"How much do you charge?"

"Oh, whatever you want to give me. I'm a poor man. I worked already at the inn for 3-4 coins per head. That will do me fine."

"Good! We'll take it!"

"Go to your rooms and I will come to you to give you the shave and the trim."

He borrowed a cake of soap, a pot of hot water and some towels from the innkeeper and went to the first man's room. He soaped up the man's head and face with a thick lather.

"Oh! I've forgotten the razor! Excuse me just a moment while I go get it." He left the man leaning back in his chair, lathered up.

Clever Peter went to the next man's room and did the same thing. He continued through the inn, lathering each man up and then leaving to find the razor. The black lye soap was strong. The men who dared open their eyes were rewarded with the sting of soap as it dripped from their foreheads. What could they do? They had to wait for the barber to return with the razor.

When he had finished lathering up the other men, he lathered up his own face, head, and beard, so no one would recognize him. Then he called out, "What is going on here? Where is that dratted barber, who left me all soapy? I'm going to get him!"

The other men heard this and leapt up to join him. The soap ran down their faces, down their necks. They ran this way and that, trying to get the soap out of their eyes, furious at having been tricked by—who else?—Clever Peter.

Storyteller's Note: Like Nasruddin Hodja, Clever Peter travels. His reputation as a trickster precedes him. In this tale, the men in a village sit around drinking coffee. This would have been sweet black Turkish coffee, brewed over coals in a copper pot with a long handle, and served with the grounds still in the cup. The first time I was in Bulgaria, I didn't know that the bottom third of the small cup would be fine coffee grounds, so I drank them and almost choked. I also learned that it's an old Bulgarian custom to read the future in the coffee grounds.

In the archives at the House of Humor and Satire, I came across this Clever Peter story. Clever Peter is always interested in making extra money.

The Car in the Mud Puddle

A traveler's car got stuck in a huge mud puddle. He went forward and back, forward and back, but only got deeper into the mud. Clever Peter and his son were resting by a tree not far off.

"How much to haul us out of this mud?" the traveler asked.

"Twenty grosh."

"What! That's far too much."

"If you think it's too much, get it out yourself."

In the end, they pulled it out and were paid their 20 grosh.

"Hmph. You're both a couple of loafers. All day you lie in the shade and then you make 20 grosh off of me."

Clever Peter's son said, "What are you talking about? We work all day and night! All day we pull cars out, all night we carry water from the river to make that mud puddle."

Storyteller's Note: I'm not sure how much twenty grosh is, but it seems that it's a significant amount. Grosh was the currency until 1882.

Of course, Clever Peter and Nasruddin Hodja are not the only tricksters in Bulgaria. As in every culture, tricksters in human form abound.

Who Are the Thieves?

An old man went to cut wood in the forest. There he found a bag of gold. He took the gold home but said to himself, "This isn't my money. I'll find out whose it is and give it back." His wife said, "That money belongs to some thieves. There are some who live in the forest, go and find them."

He found a band of men in the forest. "No, we're not thieves, we're rebels. We steal from the rich and give to the poor.

"Who are the thieves?"

"The government officials in the city, the ministers."

He took the bag of gold to the officials in the city.

They said, "Heavens, no! We're not thieves. We work for the people. Leave the money with us for a year. In the meantime, keep looking for the thieves. Check with us in a year, and if it's still here, it's yours."

The man went back to the city in a year. The government officials said, "Money? What money?"

"Ah! It's true! The government officials ARE thieves."

Storyteller's Note: I turned up this story in a folklore collection from 1918, though I heard the same kind of complaint in 1983 and 2015. In 1983, the joke I heard about the government was "they pretend to pay us, and we pretend to work."

It's rare to find tricksters who are girls, though there is no shortage of sage grandmothers and crafty women. Here's a story of a crafty girl.

Until Monday

One man lent another money. The lender went to collect on the debt many times, with no luck. One day he knocked on the door looking for payment. The man wasn't home. His daughter answered the door.

"Where is your father, little one?"

"He's not here, Uncle."

"Well, when will he repay me his debt, little one?"

"Oh, Uncle, he went to sow thorns by the side of the village path. When the thorns grow, the sheep merchants will go by with their sheep, and the thorns will catch on their wool. We'll collect the wool from the thorns, and we'll sell it at the market. Come back then, and we'll repay you."

The lender left disheartened.

That evening, when the father came home, his daughter told him the lender had stopped by.

"When did you tell him to come for the money?"

She gave him the same story.

"Why did you tell him to come back so soon?"

"Because next time he comes, you'll tell him 'next Monday,' because there is no end to 'next Mondays'."

Storyteller's Note: In Bulgaria, one may address an older man as "chicho" (uncle) and an older woman as "lelyo" (auntie), even if they are not related. In 1983, I was surprised to be addressed once by a child as "lelyo," as I was only in my 20s. It was like being called "Ma'am," instead of "Miss."

This next story is well known to Bulgarians, especially for the phrase, "Me, me, it's always me!" Banitsa is a pastry made with phyllo dough. For example, it can be sweet with pumpkin and walnuts, or savory, with feta cheese and egg between the layers. It's similar to what Americans know as Greek spanakopita, which would be banitsa with spinach. Many Bulgarians now use ready-made phyllo dough, but I watched more than one grandmother roll out the thinner-than-paper leaves for a delicious treat.

Me, Me, It's Always Me!

A father said to his children, "Tomorrow your mother will make banitsa. Who will eat it?"

"I will," said his eldest son.

"And we'll roast the pig. Who will eat it?"

"I will," said the same boy.

"And we'll cook a goose. Who will eat it?"

"I will," said the boy.

"And then we'll plow the fields. Who will help?"

"Me, me, it's always me! What about one of the others this time?!"

126

Storyteller's Note: This version of *The Little Red Hen* is well known to Bulgarians, especially for the phrase, "Me, me, it's always me!" I imagine the boy in this story is a typical adolescent.

I was thrilled to find a version of an old tale that I knew from other countries. In this story, the devils are certainly dancing the horo, that quick-stepping circle or line folk dance. The Bulgarian verb used is "play" rather than "dance."

Two Hunchbacks

In one village, there were two men with humps. One's hump was in front, the other's was on his back. They were uncomfortable and so the two men searched for a cure. One heard of a magician who lived near a well. He went to meet this magician.

He waited. And waited. And waited. Nobody came. It began to get dark, so this man climbed a tree to save himself from any wild animals.

At midnight he heard voices. A crowd of devils was gathered below the tree. They began to dance and sing.

"Today is Friday, tomorrow Thursday, ee-ha-ha, u-ha-ha." In the dance, whenever they were supposed to go left, they went right. Whenever they were supposed to go right, they went left.

The hunchback watched but finally, he couldn't stand it any longer. "That's not how it goes! If today is Friday, tomorrow is Saturday!"

"We have a guest! Climb down, sir. Dance with us."

He climbed down, though he was afraid. Still, he danced with them. He didn't correct them for dancing backward. He just followed the steps.

At the end of the evening, one of the devils said, "What will we do with this one?"

"Take his hump!" And so they did.

He ran home as fast as he could, overjoyed no longer to have a hump. In the morning, he met with his neighbor, the other man with a hump, and told the story.

"I'm going now!"

"Remember, don't turn back, no matter how scared you are. And don't correct their steps."

The other went to the same tree, climbed and waited. After dark, the devils appeared and began to sing and dance. He hopped down and they invited him to join in.

"No! You should go right! Why are you going left?" he corrected them.

"What are we going to do about this one? He doesn't know how to play!"

"Give him the other hump!"

They did and this man went home with two humps, one in front and one in back.

Storyteller's Note: This justice tale can be found in versions from Japan, Ireland, Haiti, and Spain. In the Irish version, the dancers are fairies, not devils.

In the 1980s, I found Bulgarians to be extremely hospitable. On my arrival in 1983, I hadn't planned well. I had nowhere to stay, no Bulgarian money, I'd been riding the train for three days, and I had no idea what to do. All I had was a photocopy of a telegram saying that I could study in the country for a year and there would be a room for me. It was past midnight. A man in the train compartment invited me home. Normally, I would have refused—I didn't know him, he didn't know me, and it could have ended badly. I was exhausted and not thinking clearly, so I said yes. It turned out well, though. His family was waiting for his return and we all sat up and ate stew with bread. Only later did I think about how shocked they must have been that he arrived with a young American woman. I stayed with them for three days, though that was dangerous for the family. All foreigners were required to register with the police for every night they were in the country. Western foreigners were not allowed to stay with Bulgarians without hard-to-get permission. If he had been caught, my host might have been jailed or fined. He might even have lost his job. While staying with this kind family, I saw how they helped each other and their neighbors out. I witnessed this sort of kindness repeatedly.

The Good Deed

There was a traveler heading home after a long voyage. He came upon a man who had gotten his cart stuck in the mud. Much as he tried, the man couldn't pull his cart out of the mud.

"Would you help me out here?"

The traveler needed to get home before dark, so he refused, much as the man with the cart pleaded. The traveler went on his way. He hadn't gone far when he turned back. After all, what if it had been his cart in the mud?

It took great effort to pull the cart out of the mud, and worse, it took more time. The man with the cart thanked him over and over again and went on his way. The traveler knew he wouldn't make it to his village before dark. He stopped to sleep in a field.

In the morning, he set out for his village. When he arrived, he found that his house had burned to the ground the night before.

"That cursed man with the cart! If I had been here, I might have put out the fire! I might have saved the house!"

His wife calmed him. "Never regret the good you did for the man with the cart. We are all safe, it is only the house that is burned. It was so fast, if you had been here, you might have been killed."

Not long after, the man was raking the embers of the burned house when his rake hit a metal box. He dug it out of the ground. It was full of gold pieces.

"That blessed man with the cart! If it hadn't been for him, I would never have found this gold. Thank you, sir! I did the smallest good deed for him, and see what good has come from it."

He became the richest man in the village. He rebuilt an even better house and lived well and happily with his family.

Storyteller's Note: The original end of this good news/bad news story is: "And so the old people say, 'Do right, and throw it in the ocean.'" I puzzled over that, then understood the meaning: do the right thing, without regard for any reward you may receive.

In this collection, I've tried to show a range of stories and to give an idea of Bulgarian culture from the past as well as the present. As is the case around the world, not all the stories reflect well on the culture, not all reflect badly. This final story sums it up.

Most Beautiful

A rich man sent his servant to the market to buy the most beautiful food. The servant returned with beef tongue.

"Tongue? Why tongue?"

"Because tongue can express the most beautiful of what is in the world."

The next day, the rich man sent the same servant to bring the ugliest food. The servant returned again with tongue.

"Again tongue? Why?"

"Because tongue can express the ugliest of what is in the world."

Storyteller's Note: There are versions of this story in Cuba, Thailand, and Alabama. This story works well when teaching about metaphor. It reminds me of the Kenyan story in which the poor man's wife is happy because he feeds her "meat of the tongue," as he calls stories and songs.

Resources Cited

Arnaudov, M., and Dimitur N. Osinin, eds. *Bulgarsko narodno tvorchestvo.* Sofia: Bulgarski pisatel, 1961-1963.

Karaliichev, Angel. *Bulgarski narodni prikazki*, v. 1. Sofia: Narodna mladezh, 1985.

Liubenov, P. Sv. ed. and comp. *Sbornik s razni narodni umotvoreniia iz Kiustendilsko.* Sofia: Pridvorna Pechatnitsa, 1896.

Nicoloff, Assen, ed. and trans. *Bulgarian folktales.* Cleveland: n.p., 1979.

Popov, Sava. *Khitur Petur.* Sofia: Bulgarski khudozhnik, 1974. https://chitanka.info/book/1503-hityr-petyr

Pridham, Radost. *A gift from the heart.* Cleveland: World Publishing, 1967.

Sbornik za narodni umotvoreniia, nauka i knizhnina (SbNU). Sofia: Durzhavna pechatnitsa, 1889-

Shapkarev, K. A. ed. *Bulgarski prikaski I verovaniia s pribavlenie na nekolko Makedonovlashki I Albanski.* Sofia: Pechatnitsa na "Liberalnij Klub", 1892, 1894. http://promacedonia.org/ksh_4/index.html

Stoianov, V. D. ed. *Periodichesko spisanie na bulgarskoto knizhovno druzhestvo v Sredets.* Sredets: Durzhavna pechatnitsa, 1882.

Vulchev, Velichko, ed. *Bulgarski narodni prikazki.* Sofia: Durzhavna pechatnitsa "Georgi Dimitrov", 1954.

Vulchev, Velichko, ed. *Khitur Petur I Nastradin Khodzha iz istoriata na bulgarski naroden anekdot.* Sofia: BAN, 1975.

Zdravkov, Ivan. *Khitur Petur.* Sofia: Izdatelska kushta "Pan", 2012.

Abbreviations

HHS = House of Humor and Satire (Gabrovo) archives.

IEFSEM = Institute of Ethnology and Folklore Studies with Ethnographic Museum archives.

SbNU = *Sbornik za narodni umotvoreniia, nauka i knizhnina*

1. Kotan Bey
   I found a couple of versions at IEFSEM, including Fn AIF 62.I.3 p. 471-472, as well as in SbNU XVIII, p. 215-216. Hristo Neykov also has a version in his repertoire. In a workshop I gave, a Ukrainian friend offered a version from her own country.

2. The Hedgehog and the Fox
   SbNU IV p. 157-158
   This is another I've been telling for years. I do not remember where I first found this version. I didn't realize that this was originally from the philosophy of the ancient Greek poet Archilochus.

3. Baba's Rooster
   Hristo Neykov told me this over coffee one day.

4. The Turnip
   The version most Bulgarians know was written in rhyme by Ran Bosilek. His version ends with a mouse. I confess that I don't remember where I found this particular version that ends with a beetle. I've been telling it this way since about 1993.

5. Turtle Fetches the Water
   SbNU XXI, p. 103

6. A Bone in the Throat
   SbNU XII, p. 202

7. Who Is the Best?
   SbNU IV, p. 161. See also "The mouse and the mole" in Nicoloff.

8. Language of the Animals
   SbNU IV, p. 182.

9. Wolf and Stork Open a Tavern
   IEFSEM, AIF No. 77 III p. 197.

10. The Span of a Man's Life
    SbNU II, p. 168. Also from Albena Georgieva-Angelova. See also
    "How man's lifespan was extended" in Nicoloff.

11. Granny's Bowl
    SbNU VI, p. 127. See also "A dish for your feeding" in Nicoloff.

12. Nail Soup
    Vulchev NP p. 385. SbNU VIII, p. 228

13. How a Man Won and Lost Everything
    SbNU VI, p. 126. See also "Earned and lost within an hour's time" in
    Nicoloff.

14. Alive and Well?
    Shapkarev, no. 98.

15. Whatever You Do, You Do to Yourself
    SbNU VIII, p. 202 and Karaliichev, p. 24.

16. The Sun's Wedding
    SbNU XXXII, p. 579. See also "The sun and the hedgehog" in
    Nicoloff.

17. The Neverborn Maiden
    PSp, kn. VII, p 148. See also "The unborn maiden" in Nicoloff.

18. The Basket-Weaver Prince
    SbNU XII, p. 190.

19. Tsar Troyan Has Donkey's Ears
    SbNU IV, p. 182, p. 185 and Vulchev NP, p. 198.

20. Little Clover and the Wolves
    Shapkarev, no. 103.

21. Mara Pepelyashka
    Shapkarev, no. 28 and Vulchev NP, p. 103. See also "Mara Pepeliashka [The Bulgarian Cinderella] in Nicoloff.

22. Five Donkeys
    Vulchev KhP, p. 309 and Karaliichev, p. 209.

23. Hungry Clever Peter
    Zdravkov, p. 52. See also "Sly Peter at the fair" in Pridham, as well as "Sly Peter at the fair" in Nicoloff. I heard this from friends and also saw it in a film about Clever Peter.

24. The Soup of the Soup of the Chicken
    Popov, p. 94 and Zdravkov, p. 40. See also "The uninvited guest" in A gift from the heart by Radost Pridham (Cleveland: World Publishing, 1967).

25. Clever Peter at Court
    Popov, p. 122.

26. The Village of No Cats
    SbNU VII, p. 135 and Arnaudov, v. 9, p. 252.

27. Clever Peter and the Bones
    Popov, p. 82. I also heard this from a friend.

28. Clever Peter, Dentist
    Popov, p. 19 and Vulchev KhP, p. 262.

29. Who Do You Believe?
    Popov, p. 70. Also told about Nasruddin Hodja, Vulchev, p. 210.

30. Nasruddin Hodja Is Warmed by Moonbeams
    FnAIF K.M. 1980 No. 10 II and Vulchev KhP p. 227.

31. Nasruddin Hodja at the Bath House
    I am completely puzzled. I've been telling this story for years, but never wrote down the source. I KNOW I didn't make it up!

32. Clever Peter's Cart and Horse
    Roman Rimski, my friend who plays music on the streets of Sofia, told me this.

33. Nasruddin Hodja Saws the Branch on which He Sits
Vulchev KhP, p. 214.

34. Clever Peter, Barber
Vulchev NP, p. 398

35. The Car in the Mud Puddle
HHS, Stanka Ivanova Ivanova, 5.95

36. Who Are the Thieves?
SbNU XXXII p. 571

37. Until Monday
SbNU III, p. 245.

38. Me, Me, Always Me
SbNU III, p. 245.

39. Two Hunchbacks
IEFSEM AIF N. 210 I. 1985 AG.

40. The Good Deed
Shapkarev, no. 249

41. Most Beautiful
IEFSEM, AIF No. 3 II 133, Kostadina Nikolova Taleva.

If you have enjoyed this book,
we recommend pointing your browser to:

https://www.priscillahowe.com/

www.parkhurstbrothers.com

www.storynet.org